A Voyage Remembered

Louis Féron, St. José, Costa Rica, 1934

A Voyage Remembered

By Leslie Snow

With the Memoirs of Louis Féron

Peter E. Randall Publisher
Portsmouth, NH
2014

ISBN 13: 978-1-931807-78-4
Library of Congress control number: 2013938442

Published by:
Peter E. Randall Publisher
Box 4726
Portsmouth, NH 03802
www.perpublisher.com

Distributed by:
University Press of New England
www.upne.com

Other books by the author
Leslie Snow Paintings and Drawings, 1989
Poems of Leslie Snow, 2005

Unless otherwise noted, the photographs in this book
are the property of Leslie Snow.

Unless otherwise noted, all artwork pictured was created by Louis Féron.

Jacket design, production: Grace Peirce, www.nhmuse.com

Contents

Preface

*I*t is a curious fact: when young, I was disinterested in theories. My attention focused almost exclusively on personal experience, naïve as that may be. Today, in the year 2013 and at 87 years of age, I marvel at the impressions and images stored in my brain that come into consciousness for my edification and when I need them. This phenomenon is incredible. More than ever, I feel a profound transforming quality of nature revealing the significance of living and the significance of my thirty-six years of marriage with Louis Féron.

Acknowledgments

With gratitude, the author acknowledges advice and encouragement from many who have helped her to complete this book. Thanks are due to Richard Adams Carey, Marvin Silbersher, T. Jewell Collins and also to Leslie Knowlton and Shelly Knowlton, Marnie Cobbs, and to Nancy Williams, who translated the *Memoirs of Louis Féron* from French into English.

Part 1

Memoirs of Leslie Snow

Chapter 1

Awakening

Mary L. was a lovely maid who lived with us. She grew up on a farm and had a Polish background; her boyfriend played the accordion on the radio at noon. One day, when I was four years old and Mother was out to lunch, Mary opened space by moving chairs in the living room, turned on the radio to his performance and taught me how to do the polka. It was exhilarating. This was my awakening to dance.

Across the street from our home in South Orange, New Jersey, was Marshall School. In the school yard, I saw Mickey the policeman lower the American flag and allow it to touch the ground. Twenty-five years later, a woman who worked with us came for a visit. I didn't remember her until she spoke of my coming home from kindergarten crying so deeply she had trouble calming me down to find out what the problem was. As her story unfolded, I had complete recall of the American flag touching the ground, and tears came to my eyes again.

A first-grader, with his allowance, purchased a miniature tea set for me at the five and ten cent store. Christmas morning he left it by the door, rang the bell, and ran away.

Miss Weir was my first grade teacher. She suggested that Mother have me sit on her lap with an open book to guide my reading.

Looking at the picture on the page, I related a story. Mother encouraged imagining. Frankly, I needed reading glasses, and we went to see Dr. Leiderbach in New York. After the eye examination, he asked if I liked peanuts and chocolate, "Oh yes," was my answer. He replied, "Well, don't eat them, they are bad for the eyes."

I loved to run and to leap. An athletic daddy on our street showed me how. At first, it ruined my style, but finding that I could go higher and further, I practiced over and over again, with considerable damage to the hedge.

On a warm summer evening, kids in our neighborhood were playing kick-the-can and hide-and-seek. After a while, one of the boys, a year older than the rest of us, started to throw stones at the corner lamp post globe. Two other children joined in, but the original thrower broke the globe. This ended our play and we went home; I did not squeal. The following night, a policeman came to the door and Father greeted him; Mother and I were standing nearby.

The policeman said, "Last evening, your daughter was seen with children who broke the globe on the corner lamp post."

"Who saw the breaking of the globe?" Father asked, "and who reported the incident?"

The policeman answered. "Your neighbor across the street, Mr. Hanson."

Father said, "I will speak with my daughter and get back to you promptly." Then, he ushered me into the library, the woodshed, and closed the door. "Who was there?" I gave first names, unsure of the last names. He was able to identify the families, and asked, "Who broke the globe?"

I told him.

"Was he trying to break it?"

"Oh yes, he threw many stones."

"What did you say?" I cowered and shrugged my shoulders. Looking into my eyes, he asked, "What did you do?"

Protesting, I said, "I didn't throw any stones."

"Well dear, I have to tell you that you have made a mistake. You know it's wrong to destroy property that doesn't belong to you, and it's worse being town property. You should have shown your disapproval. If you couldn't think of what to say you should have left to demonstrate your disapproval." After a pause, he said that my allowance would be discontinued.

What mattered to me was to get back into the good graces of my father. He telephoned each of the families suggesting that a contribution be made toward the replacement of the globe, which, by the way, covered a gas lamp. Prior to this event, I remember seeing a man on horseback light the lamp in the evening, and extinguish the light early in the morning.

It was 1932. In spite of the Depression, each family contributed money. I was upset that my best friend was one of those throwing stones and I tried to stop her; she said that she wasn't trying to break it. I withheld this information. The event and Father's reasoning required thought: sharing replacement cost to take pressure off the family of the boy who broke the globe, the poorest family on the block; solidarity of parents to prevent future disunity in the neighborhood; and seizing an opportunity to instruct six-year-old children and one-seven-year-old. It was my responsibility to know to stop my playmates from destroying property which they did not own, or demonstrate disapproval and to pay for my mistakes. As I write this, I recall that Mr. Hanson was a handicapped person and years later he took his own life. Father was active in the Town Hall and considered inter-related social issues. He felt that children learn best from example. The experience was and remains unforgettable.

In August of 1934 when I was eight years old, in third grade, I heard a man play the violin at this same corner. The sound was filled with great feeling. He was a beggar and he was blind. I was upset that he was blind and ran home to tell Mother; she gave me coins to put into his cap. Returning home, I let my parents know that I wanted to play the violin. Mother's face lit up. She said, "We have one," and we went to the attic to look for it. There was a violin, labeled Stanley, signed 1878, made by Freelan Oscar Stanley, one of the brothers who originated the Stanley Steamer.

From 1876–79, F. O. Stanley was the principal of a high school and a teacher in Columbia, Pa., where my maternal grandmother, Carrie Hoffer, was a student. During his years in Columbia, he made four violins and gave one of them to Carrie. He made four hundred violins in his lifetime. Carrie died in 1932 and Mother became owner of the instrument. Because I had expressed interest in playing a violin, she gave it to me. I was present with her in the living room the day she received a telegram announcing Carrie's death, and was moved by her solemnity. It was in this period that I bonded deeply with Mother, with music, and the playing of the violin.

My violin teacher, Miss Grey, had grey hair and lived in a grey apartment, and gave a grey lesson, but I persevered. With practice and effort, I progressed to third position, and memorized simplified versions of classical pieces; Mother accompanied me on the piano. Listening to Mother play the piano was one of the happy experiences of my life. After saying my prayers at night, she left the door open, and went downstairs to perform Chopin, Brahms, Mendelssohn or Beethoven. At Marshall School, I played "Dark Eyes," a Russian folk song, at sixth-grade graduation. I wanted to play Shubert's "Ave Maria," but David L., who was a classmate and neighbor, wanted to play it and succeeded.

In 1910 when Mother was fourteen, her father, a traveling salesman, was struck by a train and killed. Mother received a five-hundred dollar inheritance. She went by trolley from her home in Greensburg, Pennsylvania, to Pittsburg to buy a piano. The piano salesman asked her what kind of piano she was looking for. She didn't know, and asked if she could play something on each one displayed to find out. Her selection cost far more than her inherited money. Before leaving the store, she presented her telephone number and said, "If you can lower the price, please call me." Mr. Andrew Mellon purchased the piano but returned it months later, as he was going to Europe with his family for an extended period of time. The owner of the shop lowered the price, telephoned Mother, and—with aid of a relative—she was able to buy it. Mother played when she was happy and when she was sad. She played in church, accompanied singers in performance and entertained her friends. This Mason and Hamlin grand piano was Mother's most treasured possession, and playing it the center of her inner life.

I was second violinist in our junior high school orchestra and sat behind a darling boy, who was first violinist. The following year I went to Kent Place, a private school in Summit, New Jersey. Walking from our house through Grove Park to the Village of South Orange, where I took a train to school, I recited favorite psalms out loud. It was my secret pleasure. In ninth and tenth grade I boarded at Kent Place. Classmates teased me; why was I practicing the violin all afternoon when I could be playing basketball or hockey? Homework and my peers forced me to stop.

The violin impressed me with its sensitive sound and the feeling of intimacy and vibration that passed through my entire body. It is known to be one of the most difficult string instruments to play, requiring constant practice. I had eyesight problems and learned to overcome the stress of following the score on sheet music by memorizing the score. I learned to play by ear which freed me to concentrate on delivery. This experience was helpful fifty-nine years later when I wrote poetry and recited my poems to live audiences in New Hampshire, Maine, Massachusetts, and Costa Rica.

In the early 1930s, I went to Sunday school and became familiar with stories from the King James version of the Bible. I still have my Bible and certificates and badges marking regular attendance at Trinity Presbyterian School. Beautiful church music and myths impressed me, and the poetry of particular psalms resonated in my mind. I also remember Charlie D., a young neighbor across the street from us, who chased me around the room at Sunday school trying to kiss me.

A highlight of winter was ice skating out-of-doors to music in South Orange Park. When weather conditions were favorable, the announcement was made at four p.m. by a village horn that sounded like a cow. I was excited by the idea of learning how to skate, having seen Sonja Henie figure-skate at Madison Square Garden. My parents bought me figure skates, a black velvet skirt, a colorful jacket, and made arrangements for skating lessons at Lake Placid, New York. The timing of this activity was ideal.

One of the great memories in my ninth year was going with my parents and my older sister, Shirley, to Barnum & Bailey's Circus, also at Madison Square Garden. Emmett Kelley, the clown, made a spectacular entrance running all the way around the enormous arena, a thrill that

I can relive. After completing his tour, he stopped suddenly, looked around him, and decided to clean up the mess. Fetching a barrel, a dust pan and a broom, he proceeded to sweep as much sawdust as fast as he could into the barrel, skidding, tumbling and fumbling. He encountered enormous difficulties collecting the smallest amount and almost fell into the barrel himself. I identified with the joy of running, with the excitement of beginnings and was enchanted by the antics of the clown, but it took me years to fully value the idea within this broad comedy and the brilliance of Emmett Kelley's performance.

In eighth grade at Kent Place School, something wonderful happened. I was enrolled with two other students in a course of art history, including Egyptian, Greek and Italian painters and sculptors. I saw for the first time prints of paintings by Leonardo da Vinci (his silver-point drawings), paintings of Masaccio, of Botticelli, sculptures of Donatello, and the frescos of Michelangelo. I started to study oil painting. Three years later, in 1940, when I was sixteen years old, Father gave me a superb book, *Art Masterpieces*, with an introduction by Thomas Craven, containing outstanding color reproductions of great works of art with form, movement and space.

I was considered a mediocre student, having difficulty keeping up with my classmates, who were bright and accepted to the best colleges in the country. Where I excelled was in sports. In my junior year I became president of Maskers, our school drama club.

Afternoon ballroom dancing opened my social life. It started at Marshall School in the spring of 1937. In my teens, I attended ballroom classes held at a country club at night. Courtesy was emphasized. Delightful young men wrote me letters, invited me to the first World's Fair, to sporting events, to parties and to the theater. Before graduating from high school, I was invited to Princeton and Cornell Universities and experienced the exhilaration of dancing on spacious dance floors in New York City with the orchestras of Glenn Miller, Benny Goodman and Jimmy Dorsey, doing the foxtrot, waltz, tango and the newer dances. Young men dressed in tuxedos, and young ladies wore long flowing silk, or taffeta dresses. There was an atmosphere of grace and elegance that ended abruptly with America's involvement in World War II.

When it was time for college, Father suggested Skidmore and the Skidmore art department. There I studied English history, biology, logic that seemed to have little or nothing to do with truth, and courses in design. Psychology interested me, but I found philosophy ponderous. Life drawing, sculpture and oil painting were my preferred subjects. I took part in public debates and prepared publications.

It was necessary to clean our rooms, to serve in the dining room and to help in the kitchen. The social environment was reserved, and few parties were held. The young men I knew were drafted into the service. I received moving letters from overseas followed by news that two of my friends had been killed.

Chapter 2

Entrance

When I was a junior at Skidmore College in 1947, my painting teacher, John Heinz, asked if I had my ticket to the concert. "Concert?" I asked. "What concert?"

He said the Martha Graham Dance Company would perform at Saratoga Theater that very night. I knew nothing of Martha Graham, and mumbled something about a test the next day. He strongly admonished me to stop everything and go, even if it meant doing poorly on the test. Then he added, "This is important, and besides, you look like a dancer to me." Surprised by his remark and curious about the Martha Graham Dance Company, I went to the concert.

Appalachian Spring is the work on the program that ignited my imagination about theater. The theme was a Quaker marriage. A husband and his bride entered their newly built home for the first time. The exultation of the husband and wife, the flock of believers and the pioneer woman, had for me an immediate appeal because of the dynamic and elemental way it was conceived and performed. Merce Cunningham burst onto the stage as a revivalist with an urgency and power that I had never seen before in any theater. By intermission few of my classmates remained in the row where I was sitting. Perhaps the dancing was too strange, Aaron Copland's music too dissonant, and

Nogushi's set too stark for their taste. Here was a glowing expression of American pioneer life, reflecting piety, tenderness and inner strength. The significance of my family's pioneer history in New England united with the joyful expressiveness of *Appalachian Spring*. Prior to this performance, the only professional dancing that I had ever seen was in the movies: Fred Astaire, Ginger Rogers, or Eleanor Powell tap dancing up and down the stairs, Gene Kelly and Ray Bolger.

The next day, I joined the college dance club. Movement was based upon a system called *eurhythmics*. It was vague, but I stayed with it. In April of that year, club members put on a program of group and solo pieces. We had a full house. I made up a solo to Gershwin's *An American in Paris*. After the performance, the directress came back stage and said, "You won."

Unaware of a competition, I asked, "I won what?"

She explained, "You have won a scholarship to study with either Hanya Holm or Martha Graham in New York for one month." I was amazed, and chose Martha Graham. I had never heard of Hanya Holm, choreographer of *My Fair Lady* with Rex Harrison and Julie Andrews.

In June of 1947, I went to the Martha Graham School of Contemporary Dance at 66 Fifth Avenue and Tenth Street. There was a small entrance room, two small dressing rooms, and a spacious dance floor immaculately kept. A wonderful piano player, Ray, improvised accompaniment to the class. It was vigorous and syncopated. Looking at the dancers and comparing my image in the mirror, my body looked wrong and my leotard didn't fit. The efforts and demands placed upon us in class were intense. I was beginning to hurt everywhere and could hardly walk up and down stairs or lift my arms to eat lunch. On the third day, Miss Graham took me aside; we sat on a long bench in the studio. In her soft low voice, she said, "Miss Snow, I think it is very nice that Skidmore College has sent you on this scholarship, but they have sent you for half of the course and that is unacceptable; it is either all of the course or nothing." I didn't know what to answer. Was she throwing me out? Could I raise the money somehow? Then she said. "I would like to offer you the other half of the scholarship." Relieved, I thanked her. The next day, there was a pronounced difference in the way I was directed; everything I did was wrong and criticized. In spite of difficulties, I was beginning to enjoy the work. The girls in the dressing room remarked that Miss Graham was interested in me.

On a sweltering muggy day, a graceful young dancer from out West crossed the floor. Martha corrected her eighteenth-century hand gesture that was inconsistent with the movement of the rest of the body. On the next crossover, the dancer's hand position was the same. Martha repeated her criticism and explained why it must be corrected.

The dancer seemed to understand. On the following crossover, there was no visible change. Martha stopped the class and said, "This is a deep-seated habit that has become a part of the dancer's muscle memory. If it is possible for this dancer to make the correction, it would take easily six months of daily effort under supervision, and it would be painful." I have never forgotten this.

Well, it wasn't long before my defects showed up: my mind wandering, my sudden changes of mood and my lack of openness. Once, Martha slapped my face symbolically, and I stamped my foot. She laughed, admiring my spirit, but this was no laughing matter. It was an ultimatum—improve or leave. The dancer whose hand gesture needed correction left the school. For me to leave was unthinkable; I was challenged and under obligation. Earnestly I wanted to learn how to dance. Martha stated a fundamental truth: *movements of the body do not lie.* We were reminded that this is a professional school. The dancer comes to the school motivated; it is not the duty of the school to motivate the student. I was learning that professional dance training is strict.

It became clear to me that the dancer cannot see what he or she is doing except for brief moments facing the mirror in class and the need for correction will continue throughout the dancer's career, first from the choreographer, and later from the rehearsal director. Martha said that it takes about ten years to build a dancer's body, and I have witnessed brilliant classroom dancers unable to make the transition to the stage. Taking away the fourth wall and facing the audience is decisive. A performing artist must have good working habits to achieve strong technique in order to communicate freely to a live audience and adapt to circumstances. Unforeseen things can happen.

Something else dawned on me; it is impossible to go up—to leave the ground—without going down first, hence the *plié*. The *plié* in dance, is the bending of the knees turned out, a critical exercise. Correctly done, it permits the dancer to spring into the air, and Martha said to us in class that the way a *plié* is executed lets her know if the dancer will become a performing artist.

On my return to Skidmore in the fall of 1947, it was expected that I give a talk and demonstration showing what I had learned with Martha Graham! The event was well attended. The president of the college, Henry T. Moore, was there, and also John Heinz. I cringe, thinking about it now. How could I possibly perform well after one month of training? Well, something must have been right because President Moore sent me a fine congratulatory letter. I valued his letter as proof that I was able to rise to the occasion, and this thought had far-reaching consequences.

Shortly after graduating with a Bachelor of Science degree in 1948, I was asked to return to Skidmore to teach three courses in art each semester for one year, as Marion Pease, the head of the Art Department, was leaving on sabbatical. This was a fine opportunity, but one I rejected, because I felt the necessity of getting out into the world.

The first step taken was modest and brief. After graduation, a classmate and I rented a studio barn in Woodstock, New York, and I painted for a month. The painter Phillip Guston saw me perform a short dance that he applauded and we spoke. Mentioning that I was a painter, he responded, "Oh no, dance, there are too many painters." He added that he was through with painting objects; Guston was embarking on what became abstract expressionism. I also met Theodore Man and José Quintero in Woodstock, who soon after created a theater, the Circle in the Square at Sheridan Square in Greenwich Village, where I had an experience as a choreographer. I lived in the Village and taught painting two days a week at Bergen School in Jersey City, grades one through twelve. A teacher at Bergen, realizing that I was an artist, asked me to make an edition of fifty etchings to be used as a bookplate. This was a wonderful commission; now I had to learn how to do it.

Stanley William Hayter, leading authority in modern print

technique, had a workshop, Atelier 17, down the street from where I lived on Eighth Street. I went to see him. He felt that I was in a hurry and gave me a whirlwind tour of the shop: showing me the tools, how to make an etching, how to set the press and how to make a print, with all the dos and don'ts. My head was spinning. Serious, known artists working there looked on with amusement. He said the fee was forty dollars a month to use the studio day or night, and he reminded me to turn down the stove when I left in the evening. I worked alone at night. With great effort and frustration, I finished the edition, but carelessly left a rejected print in the wastebasket. Hayter found it and asked, "Who is doing this?" I confessed. Then he asked, "How did you do this lettering?" I answered him but was surprised by his question. He returned to France, where he had an Atelier 17 in Paris, and wrote me letters encouraging me in my work and admiring my energy. He added, "You are lucky because you have time." I took note of his comment.

Nineteen forty-nine was a beautiful year in Carmel, California, where I had my first love affair and lived by the sea. I made drawings, held children's classes in painting, and danced for my friends. I became acquainted with Edward Weston. Point Lobos was next to the land where I lived. Weston made exceptional photographs of this magnificent place. When I returned East, he wrote to me and said, "For heaven's sake, don't give up your drawing no matter what you do; you have something to say, and I feel the same about your dancing." His remarks encouraged me to form my life's vision as an artist.

After the death of Great Aunt Lettie in Carmel, and at the urging of Father, I left California and went to Europe for a month with my parents and my younger sister, Elizabeth, for *Le Grand Tour*. Sitting with her in an outdoor café in Paris, I was seized with an idea to return to New York City and train seriously as a dancer and to perform. When I enrolled at the Martha Graham School of Contemporary Dance and announced my age, twenty-four, the secretary put down her pen and said, "Either you are very good, or you are crazy."

I replied, "Perhaps it's a little of each."

Martha was looking for dancers educated and worldly enough to dance complex roles within a complex theme. She considered her dances to be plays. She was looking for dancers with a unique kind of acting ability. She had no objection to technique by itself, but to technique that distracted the audience from the drama of her plays.

While the ballet dancer strives to glide and float effortlessly, Martha believed that life itself is effort, and that drama and effort should be made artistically visible. She used the ground, inventing falls and breathtaking recoveries, and turns that increase the expressive power of the body. These had never been seen before. She understood that movement originated from the center of the body and radiated out to all of its parts. She imitated no other style of dancing. This dramatic movement corresponded with the way I was feeling, as I was breaking away from the past.

It is instructive to think about what was happening in the world at the time. This was a period of tumult—preparation and horrors of World War II, the aftermath and depression; the twentieth century was indeed one of the most bestial centuries on record. As Martha started her career in New York in the early 1920s, the French modernists were getting rid of romantic emotionalism and focusing on restraint. Europe did not have a direct influence on Martha's work, and influence from the Orient came after her aesthetic was established. She was influenced by Jungian psychology that focused on one's inner life. Martha dared to show one's inner life and this is what attracted my attention.

In the dance, it was revolutionary. She demanded participation and involvement of the theatergoer and shunned passive entertainment and cynical detachment from what was human. Music was composed for her dances rather than Martha composing dances to fit existing music. Her costumes and sets were expressive, sparse and symbolic. In this period, to my knowledge no dancer created more lasting innovations than she did, and the *Graham technique* may be her greatest contribution to the dancing art.

Her own training started at age twenty-three with Ruth St. Dennis and Ted Shawn at the Denishawn School in Santa Barbara, California, in 1916. There she met Louis Horst, a composer who became her musical director, composer and mentor. Louis and Martha were together twenty-five years or longer. In 1928, a course in choreography was created by Horst based on pre-classical forms, such as the *pavane, gavotte, gigue minuet, rondeau, bourrée* and *sarabande*. During this period, instruction was needed as dance had been relatively unstructured and cluttered with elaborate sets and costumes.

In 1952, I studied choreography with Louis Horst and he told me this story. When Martha took his course in the twenties, she ran in every dance.

He said, "Now stop that, Martha. This is a *sarabande*, a slow stately processional dance."

She snapped back, "What are you trying to do, put out my fire?"

He answered, "Never mind, dear, you will build another one."

Exactly one year after the most intensive training of my entire life, Martha phoned me at the Bergen School to ask if I would join the Martha Graham Dance Company as understudy. Naturally, I accepted. I asked her what was expected of me. She replied, "Learn everything," which I interpreted to mean learn all of the non-solo parts. I was present at every rehearsal of the supporting cast, and secretly tried on costumes, observing how much alteration a skirt would need in the event that I was called upon to replace a dancer. There were thirteen members in the troupe, and I was the only understudy.

Martha gave me two entrances in *Canticle for Innocent Comedians*, a lyrical work premiered in 1952 at Juilliard School of Music. During rehearsal, she asked us to move set pieces that had been placed behind musicians and were designed to project sound. She was exploring how they could be used in the dance. We grunted and groaned and looked like we were moving steamer trunks. Martha came on stage with her arms in the air and gave a push with her hip. The set piece moved silently as she imagined. During dress rehearsal with full orchestra, we were aware suddenly of no scrim to cross behind, enabling entrance on the opposite side of the stage. Moments later and without rehearsal, each dancer reversed her sequence, so that her exit would bring her back where she started. It worked, and Martha was impressed.

THE · PLAYBILL · A · WEEKLY · PUBLICATION · OF · PLAYBILL · INCORPORATED

WEEK BEGINNING SUNDAY EVENING, MAY 17, 1953

Gertrude Macy Presents

MARTHA GRAHAM
and DANCE COMPANY

PEARL LANG	HELEN McGEHEE	NATANYA NEUMANN
ROBERT COHAN	STUART HODES	BERTRAM ROSS
DAVID WOOD	JACK MOORE	
PATRICIA BIRSH	MIRIAM COLE	MARY HINKSON
LINDA MARGOLIES	LESLIE SNOW	MATT TURNEY

Guest Artists

JOHN BUTLER	JANE DUDLEY	MAY O'DONNELL

YURIKO, Courtesy of RODGERS AND HAMMERSTEIN

Conductor: SIMON SADOFF

Musical Advisor: HELEN LANFER

Lighting: JEAN ROSENTHAL

Martha Graham Dance Poster

The early fifties were stormy years for Martha personally, and there were several new dancers in her company. One of the dancers injured her back. A five o'clock rehearsal was called at the Alvin Theater on Broadway to prepare me to replace her in two pieces: *Night Journey*, a dramatic work based on *Oedipus Rex*; and *Letter to the World*, a beautiful lyrical work based on Emily Dickinson's poetry. I shall never forget the feeling of togetherness that took place during the rehearsal and evening performance. The Graham dancers, all of whom were distinct individuals, shared a belief in the aesthetics of this extraordinary dance theater. Many of them trained and danced together for years. They were highly skilled in both solo and ensemble work. I have never met a Graham dancer who was not transformed by his or her experience dancing in the company. It was a sensational event for me. I became a full member of the company by virtue of this performance.

MY HEART LIFTS

The sound - I hear the call
An oboe, a flute, timpani.
Musicians prepare to play
My heart lifts as the lights dim
A hush flows through the hall
Majestic curtains open
And wonderment begins.

Dancers trained and ready
Enter purged by fire.
They ignite my oldest memories—
My oldest deepest memories
Of sacred rhythms pulsing
In celebration living
Beyond mental striving
Beyond the mind's control.

Sadness has no meaning
Coiled and asleep,
I awake to leave my misery
To elevate my role-
Expanding dedication
To find a better way,
A fresh new rendering
Of inner spirit breathing
Rising above a selfhood
Like the dancers listening well
In a throbbing natural rhythm
Surrendered to the soul.

Leslie Snow, 2005

After my teaching day at Bergen School, I had a habit of stretching out on the floor of my apartment to rest before dance class. Once I awakened suddenly in a panic realizing that I would be late. I grabbed my things and flew down Fifth Avenue to Tenth Street, ran up the stairs, changed my clothes, and slid into place on the dance floor. Martha was teaching. Then something extraordinary happened. My energy level was so high that while dancing, I had the sensation of leaving my body. It was incredible. Martha remarked. "Very beautiful, Leslie." She need not have said that. I never forgot the feeling I had. Martha asked me to be a demonstrator for some of her master classes.

Dame Nanette De Valois, the directress of the English Saddler Wells Ballet, now the Royal Ballet Company, came with the company on their first tour to Canada and the United States in 1953. She came to the studio and watched one of Martha's classes that I was in. Martha introduced De Valois, who spoke of her dancers performing in London at Covent Garden in a partially bombed out building during the Second World War. They danced by candlelight in leotards that had so many darns; few of the original threads were left. The theater was packed. Her elegance and determination impressed me. Single-handedly she built a world-class company, which took twenty years to accomplish.

Another remarkable day was with Helen Keller and her companion, Polly, at Graham's sixty-third street studio. A scene was being filmed for a movie of Helen's life, which I was in. Guthrie McClintic, Katherine Cornell's husband, was there along with the English actor, Robert Helpmann. It was prearranged that Helen would be permitted to touch the bodies of the dancers. Their beautiful trim, firm bodies fascinated her. She spoke of their qualities, and her characterization on the basis of touch was exact. Helen said that everyone has a handicap and that hers happened to be blindness. I remember her saying that it was a joy to be in the presence of such excellence. Everyone present was moved; it showed in their faces.

I did not take part in the ceremony of Helen touching the dancers' bodies because shortly before, I was introduced to Helen by Nella Henney, who wrote of Helen Keller's teacher, Annie Sullivan. I think the ceremony referred to was considered more authentic without prior information about the dancers Helen touched. (Nella Henney lived for seven years in the Village of Snowville named after Joseph Snow, my great-great-grandfather, who settled in the Town of Eaton, New Hampshire, on virgin land in 1815.)

The Graham Broadway season was three weeks of the year or less. I wanted to dance more often, and opportunities presented themselves. One day, I asked Martha if she was planning to use me in her next Broadway season. Startled by my question, she replied, "I don't know yet. You are an artist, Leslie, but I am not sure that you are a dancing artist." I was upset and phoned to ask if we could talk things over. She hesitated, and then consented, and our talk was cleansing. A dancer, she explained, places dance before parents, siblings, lover, husband and children. Martha faulted me for not bonding more closely with members of the troupe. She made several complimentary remarks about my father and inappropriate remarks about my mother. Martha had a tendency to irritate her female dancers by disapproving of their mothers. I have always been sensitive to Mother's seemingly carefree remarks but was careful not to comment, as Martha had deep-seated problems of her own. Respecting her genius, I thanked her for my experience in her company. Six years later, after a performance of *Clytemnestra*, I went back stage to greet Martha. She said that it had been such a long time since I had come to the studio, but I never returned.

My performing years, 1950–63, included three years with the Martha Graham Dance Company, four with the Charles Weidman Dance Company, and four years with the Mime Theater of Étienne Decroux. Early in the 1950s at Columbia University, I danced in a ballad opera, *Acres of Sky*. At Henry Street Playhouse I performed in a duet with Paul Taylor as His Magic Chicken in *Jack and the Beanstalk*, one of his first dances. I was in Eugene O'Neill's *Mourning Becomes Electra*, realized in terms of movement for dancers by Dale Edward Fern at the Amato Opera Theater, and was invited to dance in summer stock at Cain Park Theater in Cleveland, with lead roles in *Carousel* and *Brigadoon*.

I danced with the Charles Weidman Dance Company at Dance Theater, the City Center Dance Festival, Henry Street Playhouse, Connecticut College and Jacob's Pillow Dance Festival. Charles Weidman, one of the founders of modern dance, started with Denishawn—Ruth St Dennis and Ted Shawn—and performed with Martha Graham with the Humphrey Weidman Company, and later with his own troupe.

I played in *Flickers*, a satire on the silent film; *Lysistrata*, a Greek comedy; and *The War Between Men and Women*, inspired by James Thurber. Referring to the New York premiere, dance critic Walter Terry said of my performance, "Everyone adored the identified blonde who flopped about with such supreme incompetence. She clearly joined in out of loyalty to her sex since a man's world was obviously just fine as far as she was concerned." After our Jacob's Pillow performance, Walter Terry wrote, "As a Reluctant Blonde, in the army of women, Leslie Snow gave an appealing and intensely funny characterization."

Against serious music, the fourth movement of Tchaikovsky's Sixth Symphony, Weidman achieved comic effect. He understood that people who take themselves too seriously are apt to be funny. In twelve scenes, he combined elements of seriousness and surprise with a real problem— *Women's Lib*. Walter Terry wrote. "The audience, which jammed this dance theater to the last inch of legal standing room, chuckled, laughed and roared." Each time we performed the piece, the funnier it got. Charles was in the dance. He spoke with me afterwards to try to understand why it was gaining in comic effect and carefully explained the rules of comedy. I had never heard of the rules of comedy. I wanted to be charming and amusing, not hilariously funny. When I realized that this was type-casting, I was hurt. It took me time to adjust to the fact that comedy is based on ridicule. Thinking it over, I made a decision not to perform comedy again on the stage as a dancer. While it has a place in family life and within an ethnic group where people know each other well, on the world stage it is misplaced. An international audience represents diverse backgrounds. We need sensitive awareness to unite a troubled world.

I danced in *By the Beautiful Sea* with Shirley Booth on Broadway at the Majestic Theater and later at the Imperial Theater. Helen Tameris, a former Graham dancer, choreographed the musical. She saw me perform with Weidman at Connecticut College and asked me to audition. There were three replacement openings, and about 400 dancers lined the city street waiting to audition, which took days to accomplish. I was fortunate to be accepted and played in eleven scenes with many costume changes, and had a delightful mime spot.

My first performance in this musical was an obstacle course. To save money by not activating union rules, the director gave me verbal instructions only, no rehearsal time with props and sets that malfunctioned, but after the first night it was smooth sailing. I performed with the company for a year until the show closed in 1955.

The closing of *By the Beautiful Sea* was a reminder—my dancing years were ending. Needing perspective and with the help of my parents, I traveled and worked in Western Europe for twenty-one months.

Chapter 3

A Beam of Light

In April of 1955, in New York City, I met a man of Norwegian background who was employed in the Foreign Department in Oslo. He encouraged me to visit Norway. Father was hopeful that I would consider leaving theater life. A clerk at the airport found my luggage 14 pounds overweight and waived the fee. Smiling, he said, "You look like you are getting married."

While I fumbled for change, a thoughtful young man insisted on paying the limousine fare, so I smiled and thanked him. Just as I boarded the plane, a journalist approached me and asked, "Are you Miss Snow?" He wanted a picture story, where-upon I was allowed through the gates early and stood on the runway smiling, waving a hankie. He was looking for a more provocative gesture but settled for the above.

In all my days, never had I seen a more dramatic and spectacularly beautiful sight than Norway from the air: snow, snow, snow everywhere, mountains, ravines, frozen fjords rugged and primitive; you can't believe that people actually live there. Even flying low, few dwellings and no roads were visible. Exclaiming to my seatmates, I was reassured that people do live there and get around on skis.

Soon after my arrival, it became apparent that my friend had difficulties in his personal life. I stayed at Ringköllen, a small inn near

Oslo in Hönefoss; his hut was a half-hour hike up the mountain. We met several times and were not at ease with one another. This was upsetting, but I had the address of a Norwegian family nearby, a couple with two young daughters, and I lived with them for a while. They were wonderful and the order and simplicity of their daily life helped me to regain balance.

Through new acquaintances, I learned of the availability of a flat in the middle of town owned by a horse trainer who was away. A funny thing happened. Gazing out of the window, I saw a man filming a group of people across the street. I went directly to the location, and was not only accepted as a performer in the scene being shot, but landed a one-day film job as a *nun*! The latter film was called *Unhappy Man* and was about the safety-first theme for an insurance company. First proofs were available for viewing before editing, but I never saw them, as I was preparing to leave the country.

Another occurrence was meeting Helmer B., a perfect gentleman and a survivor of five German prison camps. He had suffered, and was still enduring physical ailments. His wife was in the hospital, critically ill, with a cerebral hemorrhage. Instead of being bitter, he was kind, patient and good with people, a man of his word, and highly respected. I think he was in the underground during the war. He drove me around in his car, took me to dinner, to the Danish Ballet, and introduced me to the May 17th celebration of Norway's date of independence from Denmark in 1814. Helmer knew the man I came to see and was aware that our friendship was not developing. Helmer wanted to show me the best of Norway, and generously offered to drive me through Europe, if I cared to make a tour, but I was unable to accept his invitation.

Our last dinner together was at the Grande Hotel in Oslo. Members of the Labor Party and their wives were dining upstairs and came down later to dance. Helmer introduced me to his friends: the minister of commerce, the minister of industry, and several members of parliament. A man in the foreign affairs department who was a representative to NATO took a shine to me. He asked if I planned to stay a while in Oslo. I answered, "Yes, if I can find a job." He informed me of the state visit to Norway of H.M. Queen Elizabeth II and H.R.H. the Duke of Edinburgh on the 24th to the 26th of June. A woman who spoke good English was needed on the staff. He thought there was a chance of a position for two weeks or so before their arrival. When I expressed interest, he arranged an interview, and I was signed up at the International Press Office in Oslo to work with a Norwegian-American gal, Laila G., about twenty-seven, married to an American writer. Laila was an assistant to the man in charge of the Queen's visit from the Norwegian side. How fortunate I was to meet Helmer and Laila.

About one hundred and fifty foreign correspondents and photographers came from England, France, Sweden, Denmark, Germany, Russia, Vietnam and, of course, Norway. About eighty organizations were represented, including the BBC, Time & Life, the *Chicago Tribune*, the United Press, International News, and Fox Movie Tone. With the exception of the telephone operator, Laila and I were the only women in the office; our desks were in the middle of it. While she did most of the work, I greeted, welcomed and listened.

Between 8:00 and 11:30 a.m. correspondents and photographers came for information, press cards, telephoning and cabling. Laila and I received formal invitations to cocktail parties and dances and were invited to the lounge near the office where drinks were served. My thought was, if I accept all of these invitations, I will be swinging from the chandeliers! The Englishmen I met were bright, charming and very diplomatic.

We stood among the press at the pier with excitement, awaiting the arrival of the queen and the duke, and felt the eagerness of photographers to get a good shot of the queen's first moment on Norwegian soil. Just before their arrival, as an escort pulled up to transport Crown Prince Olav out to meet the Royal couple, one of the sailors, pushing off, fell into the drink. You should have heard the cameras clicking. It was the kind of incident the press looks for. I was impressed with how many cameramen got it, as it happened so quickly. Poor fellow, he went out to the *Britannia* dripping wet.

The queen was lovely; indeed, I admired her complexion and sweet smile and her beautiful carriage, both gracious and dignified. The Duke of Edinburgh was, as usual, delightful. For me, this was living theater.

Laila and I had passes to all events with the exception of a gala performance of Ibsen's *Peer Gynt*. While she succeeded in getting a ticket, I hesitated to even try to do so. Before all of the excitement of the queen's visit ended, the BBC director's secretary, Joy T., offered us the use of her flat in London for two weeks, as she would be out of town. When our job in the press office ended, off we went from Oslo to Bergen to New Castle to London, meeting interesting travelers along the way.

During our first three nights in London, Laila and I stayed at the Academy House, 42 Ladbrook Grove, near Piccadilly Circus. Teachers, scholars, researchers and men and women in various fields and from different countries lived there. Joy's flat was across the street and just before leaving on her two-week holiday; she gave a party, cocktails and supper. Laila and I moved in the next day. In the yard behind the apartment house, we enjoyed a square dance sponsored by the immediate neighborhood.

It was here that I met a stunning Englishman, a medical student and one of the handsomest and nicest people I became acquainted with in London. He was rather short, with black hair, big brown eyes that twinkled, very athletic looking, with a pleasing voice and a beautiful way of speaking. He was 29, and a graduate of Oxford where he studied economics, politics and philosophy—an unusual background for a doctor, I would say. After serving three years in the air force, he had trained at St. Mary's Hospital in London for two years, and was presently there on a scholarship. Three years of training were ahead of him. We met several times for dinner and the theater. Theatergoing and sightseeing, in small doses, were sheer pleasure. London impressed me as a civilized place, cosmopolitan without the noisy, harsh, frantic aspects of New York.

At the Rambert School next to the Mercury Theatre, I took ballet classes to keep in shape. Marie Rambert, a great lady in the ballet world, knew Isadora Duncan and danced with the Diaghilev Ballet. Marie's husband built the famous Mercury Theatre. I have a copy of a magazine *Dance and Dancer, Marie Rambert Anniversary Number,* dated 1955. It speaks of the Ballet Club, the first British dance company of any permanence. Their initial performance was in 1931 with Markova, Frederick Ashton, and Anthony Tudor. The associate director, David Ellis, invited me to dance at the Mercury Theatre Ballet Workshop, representing America, in an evening including dancers from Germany and France, but I declined, feeling unready for this responsibility.

At the Rambert School, I met Roberta Stuart, an American with Cherokee Indian heritage from Albuquerque, New Mexico. She invited me home for tea. Roberta and her husband, Frank, a scholar at the University of London, lived near Regents Park at Upper Harley Street, where Winston Churchill lived before he went to Africa as a war correspondent. After tea, the Stuarts, often referred to as F & R, asked me to stay for the weekend, and after the weekend, they asked me to simply stay. I lived with them for many months, and this became home base between visits to other countries. Their first child, Keith, born in London, became a sculptor.

Without fully realizing it at the time, Frank and Roberta were a vital link to the significance of my experience in Europe. During my stay, we had good conversation and memorable evenings with their interesting friends. It was here that I received a letter from Bath Academy in Wiltshire, an art college for men and women. They were looking for someone to tell them something of the work of Martha Graham and had contacted the International Theatre Institute. The Institute wrote to Marie Rambert, and Rambert recommended me. I prepared a talk and demonstration, but was totally unprepared for the Bath Academy.

After traveling by train from London to Wiltshire, a two-hour trip, there was a chauffeur in a limousine waiting at Chippenham station to drive me to the stone entrance of Corsham Court. An enormous Elizabethan mansion came into view. It was one of the treasure houses of Great Britain, built in the sixteenth century on royal property dating back to the Saxon kings. The last royal owner was Queen Elizabeth the First.

At the side entrance, a pleasant confident woman in tweeds greeted me, and we proceeded down a long corridor. Above us was a high ceiling. We passed a magnificent picture gallery, where I caught a glimpse of works by Van Dyke, Fra Filippe Lippi, Caravaggio, Veronese, Tintoretto and Rubens surrounded by glorious antiques. From time to time, concerts and lectures were held here. *I was getting nervous.* She said my talk would take place in the painting studio and would I care for a cup of tea? I gratefully accepted. We passed statuary, an elegant double staircase, and turned left into a paneled room where members of the faculty were gathered for tea. The atmosphere was informal and reassuring, and there was a cozy fire. I remember Clifford Ellis, the principal, and a sculptor, Kenneth Armitage. Afterwards, my talk and demonstration went well. The entire student body was present and their questions were sharp; they had boned-up and were testing me.

I stayed overnight in an enormous room that made me think of Emily Brontë's *Wuthering Heights*; drafts came from all directions. As it turned out, the winter of 1956 in England was the coldest in 100 years. The next day, Mr. Ellis took me for a walk in the ancient yew garden. Looking off in the direction of the peacocks and pheasants, he said, "And Miss Snow, when are you coming to work with us?" This entire event was an interview for employment as a dance teacher at the Bath Academy! I had the pleasure of teaching there two days a week for six months and commuted from London. The Bath Academy, an associate College of the University of Bristol, had been bombed during the Second World War, and was moved temporarily to Corsham Court, the home of Lord Methuen, who lived in a wing of this great house. The State Rooms and the Picture Gallery were open to the public. *The Remains of the Day* and other productions were filmed here. People helped me wherever I went in England. I admired their courtesy, their patience, and their ability to overcome the hardships of war. One night at the Academy, dinner consisted of three kinds of potatoes. No one complained or joked about the shortage of food. Their speaking theater was absolutely superb. I marveled at the depth, the poetry and suggestiveness of the English language, as never before.

An unforgettable performance was Bertolt Brecht's *Mother Courage and her Children*, at the Palace Theatre in London. I attended alone. A young man sitting next to me attracted my attention, but we did not speak. During intermission, in the lobby, he came over to introduce himself. He was a coal miner from Wales, willing to travel a distance to experience this powerful production of a play about the Thirty Year's War. He would return home the next day. After the show, he invited me for coffee, and the talk we had is still alive in my memory. The ambition of his life was to be a playwright. There were three generations of coal miners in his family, and he was trying to balance the necessity of earning his living as a miner with his desire to write plays by allocating time and alternating the two activities, three months mining—three months writing. I felt his determination. He was a realist and a dreamer. While he was impressed with Bertolt Brecht, I was impressed with him.

Laila had a job with the Mike Todd production, *Around the World in Eighty Days*, starring Alec Guinness. The head of the London office of Life international, Don Burke, with whom Laila worked, introduced me to Carl Mydans, the famed photographer, and to the humorist, S. J. Perelman, who wrote for the *New Yorker*. We had dinner together and Perelman later signed a copy of his *The Ill-Tempered Clavichord* "To Leslie, on the threshold of an astonishing and noteworthy career."

At the American School in London, at Grosvenor Square, there was an opening to teach third grade full-time. Family friends recommended me. I needed employment, as my work at Bath Academy had ended, but this particular job ruled out any possibility of performing on the stage. It was agreed, finally, that I teach American folk dancing to 132 students part-time. This worked and I was nicely paid. The headmaster, Stephen Echard, asked me to continue teaching, but a schedule related to dance was taking shape with visits to Spain, Belgium and Holland.

Suddenly, it was April. Hungry for sunshine and free as a bird for a month from teaching, I packed my bag for southern Spain and made a three-day trip on the P. & O. line to Gibraltar. The fee was $13 one-way. My dining room seatmate, a spirited English woman who taught geography, said, "Isn't it a shame about the rain in Spain: such a frightful mess traveling in the rain, and two weeks of rain are expected. Last year—"

As she rattled on with crisp facts about cloud formations, humidity and temperature readings, I changed my plan. At Gibraltar, I made the ferry crossing to Morocco and headed for Tangier. Coming into the harbor, the sky cleared to azure, setting off a dazzling strip of beach and white houses. The air was fresh and dry, and to my joy there was sun.

No sooner had I stepped ashore, when a Moor with a maroon fez hat grabbed my small bag and ran for a taxi, his white robes billowing behind. I clattered down the road in my high heels trying to stop him, without knowledge of Arabic and only one Spanish word, *olé*, and to make matters worse, no pesetas. I was obliged to tip him with my last sterling coin, a crown. As the taxi pulled up to the Bristol Hotel, where I had a reservation and intended to change my currency, a jubilant group of small boys paraded by chanting a rhythmical Arabic song at the top of their shrill voices. Had I known at the time that these were Moorish boy scouts praising Allah for stopping the rains and praying for continued sun, I would have been tempted to fall in at the rear.

The proprietor, Señor Romero, recommended by my travel agent, was a dignified and chivalrous Spaniard from Andalucía. He was amused by my enthusiasm to visit Tangier and offered, free of charge, to escort me to see Phoenician ruins, ancient caves of Hercules, sooks and bazaars. One afternoon, we went to sip mint tea at the beautiful Sultan's Palace in the Kasbah. Four musicians sang to the accompaniment of a tambourine, a violin (played like a cello), a guitar-like instrument and a drum called a *durbouka*. I was intrigued by the pottery drum, which looked like an hourglass vase. Mr. Romero asked me if I cared to buy one. Thinking it perfect for my dance classes, I said yes. We made our way through the crowded market place, brushing away flies. He instructed me to barter for the drum, or risk ruining the merchant's day. The price was 125 pesetas; I staged an expression of shock and offered 70 pesetas. After my exclaiming with arm waving, Mr. Romero quietly said, "It's time to leave." The merchant followed us to the door, presented me with the drum, I handed him 80 pesetas and the three of us were happy.

The next day, I came to my senses; my drum did not fit into my luggage. I would be obliged to carry it under my arm. It was heavy, awkward, breakable, and the paint rubbed off when it got the least bit wet. That night, in the dining room, I met a tall affable fellow with a round face; he asked me to join him for coffee in an outdoor café. This sounded pleasant, so we taxied to a central spot and watched the people go by. Among them were veiled Berber women bent over with huge loads of twigs on their backs, Moors in loose robes and heelless scuffs, Arabs, Spaniards, Frenchmen, Indians, beggars, peddlers and a profusion of shoe-shine boys. One fierce-looking fellow in Arab garb stepped out of a Cadillac with three oranges and the *New York Times* under his arm.

My coffee companion turned out to be a London archdeacon on holiday. He had a dry caustic wit and a dignified air of superiority, but the twinkle in his eyes betrayed esprit. I was tempted to bring up my drum problem, then decided to wait. The following day, I attended his Easter service in a tiny Moorish church, the only Anglican service in town. After the service, he took me to an exotic restaurant in the Kasbah. We sat on cushions and ate couscous and pigeon pie and drank mint tea. In the middle of parlance regarding the mysterious dissonance in Eastern music, I seized the moment, and asked if he would be so kind as to take my drum on his air flight back to London. Startled, he made some excuses, and then flatly refused. I was stuck with it.

Ready to move on to Spain, Mr. Romero graciously helped me through customs and waved me off. I boarded the steamer in the pouring rain, clutching my drum under my coat. Spanish customs at Algeciras was pandemonium. A distinguished looking Italian, a few feet away, was trying to tell me about his trip to Morocco. We had to scream at each other to be heard.

"Did you go to Fez? "

"Where?"

"Fez," he shouted.

"Too bad, it's very Moorish. Did you like Tangier?"

"Yes. It was fascinating, but I have a problem."

"A what?"

"A problem, I acquired this drum."

"Oh, what a lovely drum."

"But it's a problem; I can't carry it traveling. Are you going to the US?"

"Yes, sailing tomorrow for NYC. Would you like me to take it?'

"Oh, thank you."

Quickly, I handed him my drum. We became separated by goats, peasants and tourists and he shouted, "Where do I leave it?"

I yelled, "Five Sheridan Square."

It was his turn to go through the gate. We waved to each other and then he disappeared. Eight months later, I returned to New York City and the Circle in the Square. There was my drum! My friends at the theater had guessed that it was my drum and held it for me. The Italian and I had no time to exchange names, and he did not leave his name at the theater.

My next destination was Torremolinus. Two self-assured American boys from the University of Madrid were going to the same fishing village. We installed ourselves in the rear of a dilapidated bus and bumped along the coast road for hours. My new acquaintances entertained me with bullfighting stories and bits of wisdom gleaned from the Spanish character. We arrived at the fishing village, but the youths in their enthusiasm had neglected to tell the driver their stop. Luggage belonging to them was on the top of the bus under a rain sheet where it would have to stay until Malaga. Disgruntled, they continued to Malaga to retrieve their bags.

I got out at Torremolinus in a gentle rain. The first sight that caught my eye was a little barefoot señorita standing in a doorway playing castanets. I headed down a narrow winding cobblestone road to the sea. Donkeys loaded with esparto, a grass used in making sandals and baskets, passed. Everyone moved slowly and noiselessly. The stillness was beautiful, and there was a smell of olive oil and pinion.

The pension was at the foot of a steep cliff on the beach of the Mediterranean. There were gypsies living in caves in a nearby cliff, and with superb luck I met a Spaniard by the name of Edwardo Felente, an author and writer of gypsy life. He held a gypsy wedding in his villa and invited me. The wedding party consisted of the bride, a wild beauty of sixteen, with full lips and a fine figure; the groom, a wiry man with demonic eyes; eight men and women of different ages; and two babies, all of them strong and strangely beautiful with poignant faces and disarming assurance. They wore ragged clothes accented with bits of color, and tattered espadrilles.

On arrival, they immediately burst into ecstatic flamenco, snapping their fingers, stamping intricate rhythms, and singing with rasping voices. Their merry-making went on into the morning with a pause for supper, sips of wine, and, of course, the wedding itself—a blood wedding, conducted by a gypsy woman acting as priestess. It is brief, and completely private among gypsies.

At one point in the evening, the groom asked me to dance. The intensity and excitement radiating from my partner enabled me to improvise and keep up with him in timing, much to the amusement of his friends. I liked these people. They had fresh direct energy, and I wished that I could understand their language.

One of the guests at this wedding party was a strapping Princeton graduate, Ricardo V., on an extensive tour of Europe traveling by motor-scooter. A day or so later, he asked if I needed a ride to the *feria* at Seville. This was a great opportunity, because traveling by scooter is the most fascinating way to see the country, and experiencing the *feria* turned out to be the high point of my experience in Spain. The scooter, an amazing machine, goes 140 miles to the gallon and can carry as much as 400 pounds of luggage, plus two people. Since the roads we traveled on were poor, speed was not always possible or desirable.

We made a short visit to the Alhambra Palace in Granada in the Sierra Nevada mountains and after that, went directly to Seville. What an indescribable pleasure to pass in miles of countryside rich in terra cotta, burnt sienna, chestnut and red, and to drive through little villages of white adobe houses, where young girls carry water from the well and women scrub clothes on stones and let them dry in brilliant sun. Children crowded around the mysterious scooter. Everywhere we stopped, people were friendly and dignified. We bought traditional refreshments—wine, bread, cheese and fruit—and sat under an olive tree to eat lunch.

When we reached Seville, the *feria* was in full swing. This was the gayest, most spontaneous celebration I have ever experienced. For five days and nights, the Spanish people rejoice with the coming of spring. It is a pagan fair and a dancer's paradise. In the center of the city, streets are lined with cozily furnished enclosures with three walls, leaving a stage for public view. Schools, churches and other organizations rent these enclosures for their members, who get up to dance while the guitarist plays and the onlookers clap and sing. The entire city is dancing—in the streets, on the sidewalks, in the café—and within this celebration there is form. A gypsy, with a gesture, invited me to dance. With a gesture, I accepted and a small gathering immediately encircled us clapping and singing. I felt in each piece a beginning, middle and an end, and after a series of three pieces, the small group dispersed. Next a proud cavalier rode on horseback dressed in tight trousers, short jacket and a broad black hat. Sitting behind him sidesaddle was his Señorita, in a ruffled polka dotted skirt, bodice and shawl with a rose in her hair.

Every evening at 6:00 p.m. the bullfight began, and it seems to be the only occasion in Spain that begins on time. It was impressive for its color and pageantry and for the skillful and beautiful movements of the matador; an exciting show, but one evening of six fights was enough; the goring of the horses by the bulls was too much for me.

Hotel accommodations were expensive and hard to find. I was fortunate to meet an American who let me sleep on her living room floor. During my three-day visit, I had but a few hours of rest. I will never forget a man standing under a tree by himself playing small castanets and singing his heart out at three in the morning. When I walked by the next day, he was still there, singing. I left the *feria* of Seville uplifted by a celebration so passionately expressed in flamenco music and dance.

Managing a ride to Cordoba, I took a ramshackle train to Madrid. Seven travelers sat on wooden benches bumping knees with other members of the small compartment. Our train broke down in the middle of the night; we waited for hours while the missing bolts and screws were replaced. It was a chance for me to learn some Spanish. Fatigued and six hours late, we arrived in Madrid. Mr. Romero's wife, Carmen, who was visiting her mother, guided me into this breath-taking city.

At the Prado Museum, one of the greatest, I focused intently on three painters: El Greco, Velàsquez and Goya. Goya's *The Third of May* was very moving. I marveled at *The Three Graces* by Rubens, *Venus and Adonis* by Veronese, *Self-Portrait* by Dürer, and *The Descent from the Cross* by Roger van der Weyden. What an experience!

Afterwards, ready to travel, I took the modern Talgo express to France and changed trains at the border for Paris, where I chanced to meet a couple of touring flamenco dancers. They had just come from Madrid, where they went once a year to be re-costumed and re-shod. I found them elegant and warm-hearted and was happy when they asked if I was a dancer. We had such a lively time together that I changed my ticket from Paris-Dieppe to Paris-Calais to be with them. In our compartment, there were two Texan ladies with fancy luggage, an Arab from Bagdad, and my new companions, Señor and Señora Vazquez. They brought out exquisite, fifty-year-old castanets and a small pair held on the thumb, played by snapping the first finger against it. The intricate technique of hand-clapping and heel-stamping was explained and demonstrated. Down came the guitar off the rack, and we sang and clapped our way to Calais. From Calais to Dover, from Dover to London, pleasantly refreshed, and warmed through by the change, by the people, and by the sunshine. I was ready to dance new life into my job.

On my return to London, I wrote to Ivo Cramer, a choreographer from Sweden, well known in Europe, to ask him if he would be willing to create a piece for me to use in auditions. He sent a telegram right away and came to the Mercury Theatre. We had a delightful time working together. I performed my *Opus one half* and a piece entitled *Bach Interlude*. Cramer seemed to enjoy these works and gave me valuable criticism. He outlined a new dance, refusing payment, and then suggested that I contact Albert Mol, a great performer in Amsterdam. Cramer spoke of Wim Sonnefelt, a well-known producer in Amsterdam, whose style and interests were in keeping with mine.

My first stop was Belgium where I stayed with the family of a young banker, Marcel K., twenty-one years of age, whom I met at the Academy House in London. He composed appropriate music for several of my dance pieces and we planned to perform together in Brussels and Amsterdam. Soon after, I realized that dear Marcel had serious emotional problems and was unreliable as a performer. We had to cancel our project, and I was disappointed because he was skillful and sensitive. In Amsterdam, Albert Mol met me at the station with a bouquet of yellow tulips. What a charming man. I was at ease in Holland after the serious and somewhat oppressive atmosphere of Belgium, but I enjoyed my visit to Rubens' home in Brussels and to the beautiful historic Antwerp.

Albert watched a class that I took at Nell Rose School of Ballet. He could see that I was relatively untrained in ballet technique and arranged that I teach a class in modern dance, which interested Albert and showed what I was able to do well. He then choreographed *The Afternoon of a Woman* for me, and we had a great time. It was clear that visa limits could upset scheduling if I joined his traveling troupe. Albert and Wim had performances planned long in advance in Holland and other northern countries. After ten days in Amsterdam filled with socializing and theater, I returned to London.

Frank and Roberta informed me that John Skolle would be visiting them before returning to the United States. John was born in Leipzig into a traveling circus family from Bohemia, a fact that sparked my imagination. His father, formerly an acrobat, urged him to study at the Academy of Fine Arts and at the University of Leipzig. John became a creative artist and a writer and a friendship developed between us that is memorable.

John's first book, *Azalaï* (the gathering of the camels) was published by Harper & Brothers in 1955, an account of adventure and discovery among the tribes and caravans of the unexplored Sahara.

When I met John at Frank and Roberta's apartment in London, he was headed for Zanzibar and wrote me letters from Cairo in Egypt, Mombasa in Kenya, Tanganyika, Zanzibar, Uganda, Nairobi, Aden, London, New York, Santa Fe and Houston; altogether more than 100 letters over a period of five years, 1955–1959, and I have kept them. Once, he requested that I send copies of particular letters to help him recall details for a book he was currently working on:

Santa Fe, March 22, 1956

"—I was very much impressed by your career and would love to see some of your dance pictures. Apropos of Holland: I used to know a poet in the South of France by the name of Roland Hoist who, among other things, translated Shakespeare into Dutch. Also, my happiest business relations were with a publishing firm in Amsterdam for which I did book illustrations before the war, Of course, my main function was to be a creative artist—until writing became a greater challenge to me than painting. If one can afford it, painting really is wonderfully relaxing. One can actually go into a beautifully abstract dream doing it, whereas writing is rather hard on the nerves and brain-cells, because with sufficient technical skill form and colour almost automatically fall into place under an aesthetic impulse, while writing always demands meaning and rationalization, even in a description of the vaguest of moods or a statement of the most elusive thought. There are no such things as "happy accidents" which are quite acceptable in painting. In writing, one's sense of selectivity has to be alert and critical at all times in order to achieve a pertinent and economical expression. Yet in another sense painting is more static and concrete. The image is fixed by the material application of the paint. Interpretation is limited by a given form. In writing, there is a vast orchestra at one's disposal of infinite complexities: veiled hints, sly inferences, considered doubts, questionable certainties and dubious facts."

August 3, 1957

"Thank you so much for your wonderful letter. You really are such an altogether exceptional person that it makes me feel quite ashamed to be so completely up in the air, to be lured by a phantom when you have proved yourself so real and so generous time and again. I love you and respect you tremendously; I do so want to see you."

In 1957, I went on a safari in Yucatan, Mexico, with John and Charles Gallenkamp and Charles's girlfriend. Charles was writing a book *Maya, The Riddle and Rediscovery of a Lost Civilization* with photographs by the author and drawings by John Skolle. It was a very exciting time. At a critical moment in the jungle before sundown, John sensed that our guide had made a wrong turn and was lost. He stepped forward tactfully and took the lead. Shortly after, we met an aborigine in a loin cloth, carrying a rabbit in his sack. John greeted him with gestures and asked directions to leave the jungle. The native answered with expressive gestures. The clarity of exchange without language impressed me. Light was rapidly failing, and it was understood that once the sun goes down in the bush, it is pitch black. We got out just in time.

Soon after the Yucatan trip was completed, I felt the need to be with my parents. My father was ill and he died of cancer in Snowville, Eaton, New Hampshire, on August 15, 1958. It was a very emotional time, and I stayed with mother in South Orange, New Jersey, for some months. Needing work, I started a business venture called, *A World in New York*, for a group of sixteen-year-old girls living in suburban towns in New Jersey. This lifted my spirits and was warmly received by the girls. We met on alternate Saturdays over a twelve-week period for two seasons. The purpose was to stimulate interest in cultural events in New York such as dance, painting and music. The World in New York tours included, for example, a visit to a museum, or a circus performance and visit to the circus backyard, an opportunity to meet outstanding performers, to hear lectures, experience interviews and to have luncheons in a variety of restaurants.

On the day devoted to natural science at the American Museum of Natural History. John Skolle agreed to join us in a Taiwanese restaurant with exotic music and spoke to the girls of his experiences in the African desert. They were fascinated and one of them was absolutely transported when she learned that a blind man led the camel caravan from Taoudeni to Timbuctoo. Her mother wrote, "This is just a note to tell you that Barbie had one of the most exciting days of her life! She admires you so much and was entranced with the explorer. Her horizons will be much broader after these Saturdays with you."

One of the last letters I received from John Skolle was on May 19, 1959: "I often think of you as an ideal companion and miss you. Most women, at least the ones I meet are such awful bitches when they aren't just plain stupid, and I instinctively shy away from the arrogant and demanding American variety. It is purling to me that you are so exceptional. I still don't understand how you could be so self-possessed and gracious when we had to part in Houston. I ought not to have let you go. But then I had absolutely no money. Yet you could have easily made a scene and of course I really wanted you to come with me. I suppose you couldn't possibly think of coming out to Santa Fe sometime during the summer if I could raise some funds?"

What interfered with our relationship was the reality that John was a nomad by nature and he had difficulty supporting himself. It was neither possible nor desirable for me to support him. What I learned about his intelligence as an artist and a writer and about myself during this vital period of transition in my own life prepared me for important experiences to come.

Chapter 4

Power of Mime

A friend informed me of a lecture-demonstration on the mime by Étienne Decroux, teacher of Marcel Marceau and Jean-Louis Barrault, and I attended. In Paris, between 1925 and 1946, Decroux had appeared in sixty-five stage presentations and thirty-five films. I saw him in a beautiful film, *Les Enfants du Paradis* with Barrault, who became the head of the French National Theatre. Decroux was invited to teach mime at the Actor's Studio, the New School for Social Research, and New York University. Fascinated by the idea of mime, I enrolled in a class to be given in his studio on Eighth Avenue. Decroux's newer style, called *corporeal mime* to distinguish it from *masked mime*, was, according to Alvin Epstein (a former student of Decroux in Paris), "based upon the natural rhythms of all things that move, from trees in the wind to workmen at their labors. He sought to make gestures as ordered and rigorous as the words of a poem."

Decroux spoke no English. Everything I learned from his teaching was through his own gestures or through a translator present in class. Long before entering theater life, I was impressed by the depth of communication possible between two human beings through movement of the body without speech, and this principle was demonstrated to me over and over again during my travels in Western Europe and in Yucatan.

Vigorously I trained, and performed in 1959 with the Mime Theater of Étienne Decroux, off-Broadway at the Cricket Theater. In his review, Tim O'Connor wrote. "They proved the body unadorned can be moved in a manner that is little short of poetry in motion."

After the performance, several members of the audience came back stage. It was here that I met Louis Féron. He spoke to me in French, and I understood him to say that he met Decroux in Paris in the early 1930s. Féron telephoned to greet and congratulate Decroux, who mailed back tickets to the show at Cricket Theater. Later on I learned that Féron came to the United States in 1945, became an American citizen in 1951, and was a practicing goldsmith, jeweler, and sculptor with a workshop on Fifty-fourth Street between Seventh and Eighth avenues, a few blocks from the Decroux's studio. He came often to watch our rehearsals.

Leslie Snow and Michael Coerver, 1955. *Mime Theater of Étienne Decroux.*

Paraphrasing Decroux, mime is independent of music, scenery, props, speech and lighting. It is neither pantomime, which tells a story with gestures, nor is it dance, which may tell a story but is more general in meaning and more up in the air than mime. By comparison, mime is horizontal and closer to the earth. A dancer goes for a walk for the sake of going for a walk. A mime goes for a walk having a destination. A mime is essentially an actor. The special power of mime is silence. It is subtle, expressing inner human experience. It can be comic, tragic, poetic or dramatic, and the final effect of the greatest mime is simplicity and a universal purity. It is profoundly specific.

Leslie Snow and Michael Coerver are seen in "The Mime Theater of Étienne Decroux," opening for four weeks at the Cricket Theater Wednesday, 1955. *World Telegram and Sun Feature Magazine Section.*

Leslie Snow as mime, 1955.

The following is a quotation by Alvin Epstein:

> "Mime has always existed in the theater, either as an independent art with its own laws and techniques, or as an indispensable part of the speaking actor's tradition, and again as the dancer's means of dramatic expression. Étienne Decroux has done more than any other actor to re-establish this infinitely rich and fundamental art as an autonomous branch of theater. His thirty year study of movement has animated what appears to be a new form but is really the old reborn. This is not dancer's movement, nor acrobat's, not the old gamut of Pantomime gestures and grimaces, but the natural trajectories and rhythms of all things that move. True pantomime tradition had disappeared with the 19th century: nothing was left but some rather harmless posturing in Pierrot 'style' with facial expressions and hand positions to match. But here in this silent and sculptural world of unclad bodies moving to an internal rhythm was a reminiscence of something far grander, harking back through the *Commedia dell'Arte* to Greek antiquity."

On April 9, 1960, I attended an evening performance of *The Trees* by the Étienne Decroux Mime Theater on a program with two films: *Twilight Crane* and Edgar Allan Poe's *The Telltale Heart*. This was at Finch College Theater on East Seventy-eighth Street. I was a member of the audience waiting for a friend who was late. Louis Féron was present and came over to sit next to me. My date arrived just before the performance began. Apologizing for being late and observing Louis sitting next to me, he said that he felt that he was in the wrong place and left. It was strange behavior. Louis took my hand and held it firmly; the feeling conveyed was convincing. After the show, I returned home.

Our mime troupe continued to perform and one day, Dick de Rochemont, head of *The March of Time* in New York, proposed having a film made of Decroux's work and suggested a filmmaker, Marcel Rebiere. Dick de Rochemont became one of the sponsors. The shooting of the film took place, if I remember correctly, in the Ziegfeld Theater on Sixth Avenue near Fifty-fourth Street. When the movie was finished, *in the can* as the expression goes, there was a knock on my dressing room door. I opened it and there was Louis Féron. We greeted one another with mime and I invited him to come in. He sat next to my dressing table where jars of make-up lined a cloth, and on the cloth he drew a ring. I was startled, and thought he was fresh, but regretted later not keeping Louis' sketch. I did accept his invitation to dinner at a restaurant on Fifty-third Street; we sat side by side, European style. He spoke French and I was unable to understand most of what he said, but his gestures were clear to me. The dinner was delicious and the atmosphere pleasant. From time to time we met on Thursdays for lunch with one or two of Louis' friends who spoke French and English, and had a nodding acquaintance with diners who frequented this rendezvous, the Saint Dennis Café, which we called Sandi.

Louis was full of life. He invited me to his studio on Fifty-fourth Street and I met his secretary and several craftsmen working at their benches. Louis showed me his work in progress, finished work, photographs and his hand-made tools. I realized from the start that he was dedicated and disciplined. Every other week or so, we had luncheon at Sandi restaurant with friends. Slowly his English improved and we were able to have significant discussions about his trade. These discussions were vital to our mutual understanding and opened a relationship that surpassed anything I had ever experienced.

We talked about the meaning of the word *orfèvre*. Traditionally, an *orfèvre* was a master craftsman of a trade that included sculpting, goldsmith work, chasing, jewelry making and many related skills. He was master of his own shop aided by companions and apprentices whom he had trained. The customer came directly to the *orfèvre*, who was able to design and make the piece from start to finish. Although he worked principally in metals—gold, silver, copper, tin, iron, steel, bronze, brass, aluminum, nickel, lead and platinum (circa 1890)—he also carved ivory wood, stone, and stucco, and utilized cement, terra cotta, wax, plaster and clay. He was in command of many techniques: refining, chasing, cutting stones, setting stones, making jewelry, engraving, making medals, polishing and gilding. With the exception of cutting stones, Louis was familiar with each of these techniques. All of this was a revelation to me.

He said that for six to seven thousand years, *orfèvres* shaped and decorated objects for religion, art and everyday life. They created sacred objects used in magic and religion, art objects, vessels and tableware, cooking utensils, sewing tools, tools for science and medicine, buttons,

Leslie Snow and Michael Coerver (top) and Leslie Snow and Sterling Jensen (bottom) in "The Mime Theater of Étienne Decroux."

buckles, jewelry and personal objects (worn or carried), trophies, regalia and ambassadorial gifts.

Louis spoke of the trade of the *orfèvre* flourishing all over the world in varying degrees of sophistication until the nineteenth century, when, in commercially developed countries, the power press and the spinning lathe came into common use. Machine-made production came in to direct conflict with hand-made creation. Master craftsmen were no longer in demand. There were few craftsmen left and they were not being replaced. The masters needed to train apprentices were gone; consequently, the genuine *orfèvre* artist-craftsman had all but disappeared from our world.

I asked him about the role of the *orfèvre* in the twentieth century. He said that he was a metal craftsman who refines the shape of a machine-made object of copper, silver or gold. The piece is designed elsewhere and cast, stamped by a power press or shaped by a spinning lathe. To find a twentieth-century *orfèvre* capable of shaping metal by hammer from flat sheet metal was rare. After the *orfèvre* refines the shape of the object by hammer or solders pieces together, he sends the object to be decorated and finished by other craftsmen: chasers, jewelers, lapidaries, setters, engravers, enamellers, polishers, gliders, gold platters, ivory carvers, stone chasers and the like, depending on the nature of the object. He then assembles or mounts the parts of the piece and delivers it to his customer who is a salesman, a reseller of orfèvrerie. The *orfèvre* might work alone in his own shop with two or three workers, as Louis did, or he could be found in an industrial workshop or manufacturing concern.

We talked about the guild system, which lasted about 1,000 years uninterrupted in France, longer than in any other nation in Europe. He explained the role of the guilds that protected the level of craftsmanship in the trades in France up to the French Revolution. If an apprentice graduated to a *companion*, he was expected to make his *Tour de France* working under masters in different towns and cities of France gaining comprehensive knowledge of his trade. The guild provided him with a *little black book* containing the companion's credentials. When this artisan decided where he would like to start his *Tour de France*, the guild contacted "a mother" in that area. She was carefully selected by the guild. She had a boarding house and fed him, took care of his clothes,

Leslie Snow and Michael Coerver, "The Mime Theater of Étienne Decroux," New York 1955.

and kept a weekly report of his conduct, which she marked in his book of credentials. Sometimes the *Tour* lasted ten years. If a companion wished to try to become a master, he must achieve a *chef d'oeuvre*, a master work. He submitted a piece to be judged by guild masters. If it was accepted as a *chef-d'oeuvre*, he could open his own shop. He then trained apprentices, some of whom became companions and made their *Tour de France*. Louis said the guilds were strict and at times abusive, which gradually led to dissatisfaction. By 1789, the French Revolution abolished the authority and privileges of the guilds. Any artisan could open a shop if he had the money to do so. The careful selection of superior craftsmen and the quality of their craftsmanship gradually gave way to the power of money. The craftsman's pride was in danger of being lost. During his training in France, there were some trades, like the goldsmith's trade, which practiced guild traditions voluntarily and vigorously.

Shortly after World War I, the French government organized a national contest for trades with guild traditions, which would be held every five years. It was an effort to restore quality and to revive the craftsman's pride. The contest was open to French-speaking countries such as Belgium and Switzerland, as well as France. A title was awarded to the best craftsman of each trade and named Meilleur Ouvrier de France. For a craftsman to be eligible to enter the contest, he must have already won five or six first prizes in his particular métier.

The first title of Meilleur Ouvrier de France in chasing was won by Mr. D. Simon in 1923. In 1928, Mr. M. Doumenc received the title. Both men submitted figure and ornament chasing and each was over sixty years of age when he won. In 1933, Louis Féron won the title, Meilleur Ouvrier de France, submitting figure and ornament chasing and original hammered sculpture. He was thirty-two years of age. His work represented six separate trades in France: ornament chasing of bronze casting, figure chasing of bronze casting, ornament *repoussé* chasing, figure *repoussé* chasing, sculpture "au marteau" (hammered over anvils) and *orfèvrerie*.

I could see that Louis was realistic about changing times. Rapidly approaching was a way of life dominated by the machine. Handwork was taking a smaller role and in the process of disappearing. The Great Depression closed the workshops in his trade, and he was the last craftsman employed in the Delsinne shop in Paris. To compete with his boss was unthinkable. He went to London looking for work, but there were no opportunities. The effects of the Depression in London were worse than they were in Paris. It was necessary to find employment, and with the war approaching, it was time to leave Europe. On December 29, 1934, Louis sailed from South Hampton, England to the United States on a merchant ship with few passengers over rough seas, a prolonged and difficult journey.

In New York he found long bread-lines. He felt the Depression was worse in this city than it was in Europe, and conditions made it impossible for him to start a business. He had a recommendation from Monsieur Rivet, the director of Musée de l'Homme in Paris for the Costa Rican government. Louis took a boat of the United Fruit

Company, *Le Petain*, to Costa Rica where he worked for eleven years under four Costa Rican Presidents.

Before speaking of our life together, it seems best to go directly to Louis' memoirs; he wrote them in French and they were translated into English in 1998. Louis loved life and he believed in himself. His memoirs contain breath and spirit of the man, the artist and the craftsman.

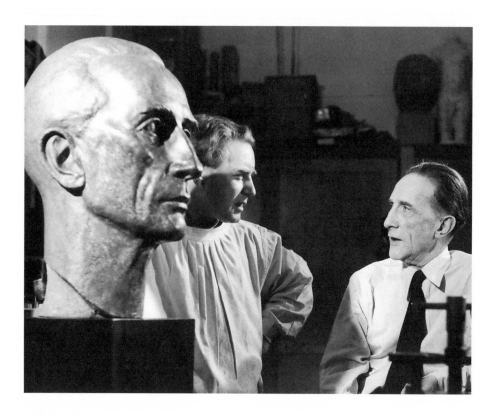

Portrait of Marcel Duchamp, 1950, over-life-sized portrait of the painter, Marcel Duchamp, modeled from life. Made in New York. *Les Collections Nationales France. Musée d'Art Moderne, Paris.* (Photo shows Féron speaking with Duchamp, while making portrait.)

This image ran in the King Features Syndicate under the headline "The Complete Artist" with the following text: "His friends called France's great artist, Louis Féron, the "modern Benvenuto Cellini," but he can create things which didn't even exist in Cellini's time. Over a garage in midtown Manhattan, Féron has a small business where objects of art are wrought for the church. Féron is not only a sculptor, but a fine goldsmith, jeweler and engraver. His works are in collections in Costa Rica, France, Spain, and Panama. He has been honored by more governments than any other living artist. He has also won grand prizes dating back to 1929. His unique reputation lies in his ability to work in copper, bronze, stone, cement, silver, gold, platinum and inlay wood. He is, moreover, that rare artist, the one who sees the rough conception through to the finished product in media for the most part unknown to the most skilled U.S. specialists."

PART 2

Black and White Photo Gallery

and

The Memoirs of Louis Féron

Louis Féron—Curriculum Vitae

*L*OUIS FÉRON (1901–1998) was a practicing goldsmith, jeweler, and sculptor. Born in Rouen, Normandy, France, and educated in Paris, he apprenticed and worked in Volk Bronze Figure Workshop as a figure and ornament *ciseleur*. He apprenticed and worked as a gold and silversmith in Atelier Delsinne, 1924–1933, earning a master's salary at age twenty-five. He served two years in military service.

Féron entered major competitions, winning distinguished awards and the title *Meilleur Ouvrier* de France in 1933 as best *ciseleur* of France for a goldsmith work entitled *Head of Jean*, now in the permanent collection of the Boston Fine Arts Museum. He was named *Commande De l'ordre du travail* by the French government and decorated in the Sorbonne. In 1934, he was awarded the bronze medal by the *Society Des Arts, Sciences et Lettres*. Féron left France in 1934 and opened his own workshop in San José, Costa Rica, where he designed and executed sculpture, jewelry and goldsmith works for the church, government and private customers.

In 1936, he was appointed by the Costa Rican government to organize and direct an apprenticeship School of Public Works in San José. He was cultural attaché of the French legation of Costa Rica until he became secretary of propaganda to the Free French in 1941. In 1945, Féron came to the United States and opened his own workshop. He became an American citizen in 1951. He designed and executed sacred vessels, objects of art, jewelry, and sculpture for private customers and for the following houses: Rubel, Van Cleef and Arpels, Verdura, Schlumberger, Bronzini, Cartier, David Web, Tiffany & Co. and Steuben Glass. His work was accepted in the collections of: Musée d'Art Moderne, Paris; Museum of Fine Arts, Boston, MA; Currier Museum of Art, Manchester, NH; the Virginia Museum, Richmond, VA; and the Cathedral of Detroit, MI.

Féron received an honorary degree, *Doctor of Humane Letters* in 1977 from Plymouth State College of the University System of NH and a citation from the government of Costa Rica in 1987 for his "great contribution to the artistic and cultural heritage of the nation." From October 1995 through February 1996, thirty-five works made by Louis Féron for Schlumberger were exhibited in Paris at *Musée des Arts Décoratifs, Palais de Louvre*.

Head of a Woman, 1974, hammered and raised seamless from a single sheet of 22 kt. gold. Mounted on an ivory collar with gold ornaments. Verde antique marble base. Marks: Louis Féron 1974. Height: 10 ¼ in. *Purchased by Dr. Frank Reed. Permanent collection of Portland Museum of Art, Portland, Maine.*

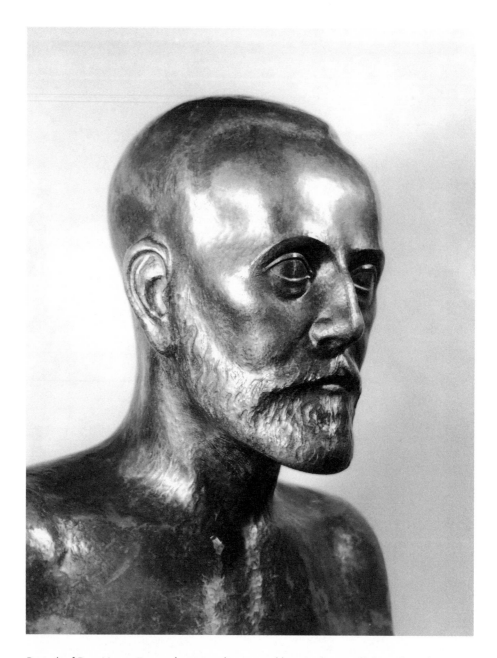

Portrait of Don Mauro Fernandez, 1937, hammered bust in the round (seamless) by Louis Féron from a single sheet of half-red copper and chased au repoussé. Height: 24 in. *Commissioned by Señor Umana for the Colegio de Señoritas, San José. Owned by the Republic of Costa Rica.*

Espoir, 1975, sterling silver, 22 kt. gold, turquoise, emeralds and chrysocolla. Depicts a human hand hammered and raised in sterling silver with a sleeve chased, ramoleyé, trace mate, and trace descendu. The hand is holding an egg of chrysocolla stone ornamented with 22 kt. gold flames and set with turquoise studs; the sleeve embellished with three cabochon emeralds set in gold. The whole set on an oval rosewood base. *Private Collection.*

Chalice, 1951, silver gilt. Hammered, raised and worked in repoussé. An alternating wheat and grape motif decorates the cup. The node has six facets with monograms of Christ and the Virgin and symbols of the four Evangelists. The foot bears a medallion of the Crucifixion. The paten has a central medallion of the Resurrection and a diamond below. Height: 9 1/8 in. *Commissioned by Reverend Robert J. Conlin.*

Indian Head, 1945, direct carving in granite. Made in Costa Rica and given to Nelson D. Rockefeller by Féron as a gesture of thanks for helping him to obtain a visa to the US in the 1940s.

Louis Féron, artist and craftsman in his New Hampshire studio, 1966.

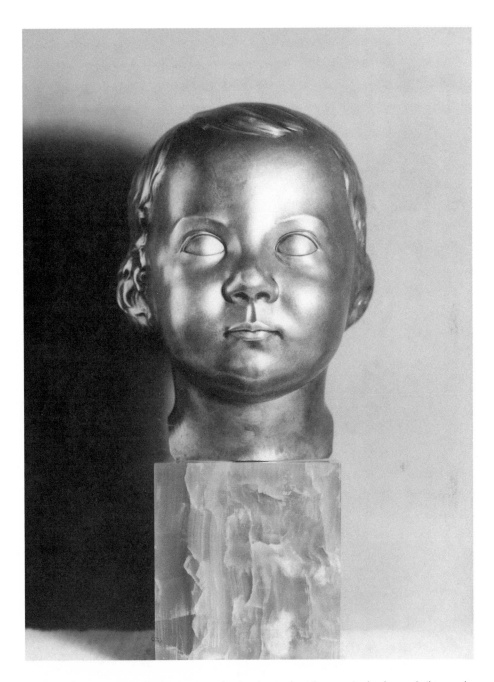

Portrait of Jean, 1930, silver. Hammered, raised seamless from a single sheet of silver and worked in repoussé; onyx base. This piece was awarded the Lepine gold medal in Paris, 1931. It also won the artist the privilege of entering the national competition organized every five years by the French government for trades with guild traditions. In 1933, together with a bronze goblet, it secured for Féron the title of *premier ciseleur-orfèvre de France.* Marks: Louis Féron 1933. Height: 8 in. Collection of the Museum of Fine Arts, Boston.

Torso, 1958, ivory, direct carving. Made in NY. Height: approx. 7 in. *Collection of C.R. Davis.*

Manila Crosier, 1954, carved ivory crosier with round silver node set with amethysts and rubies. Made in NY. *Commissioned by Cardinal O'Hara, Philadelphia, for a Bishop of Manila, the Philipines.*

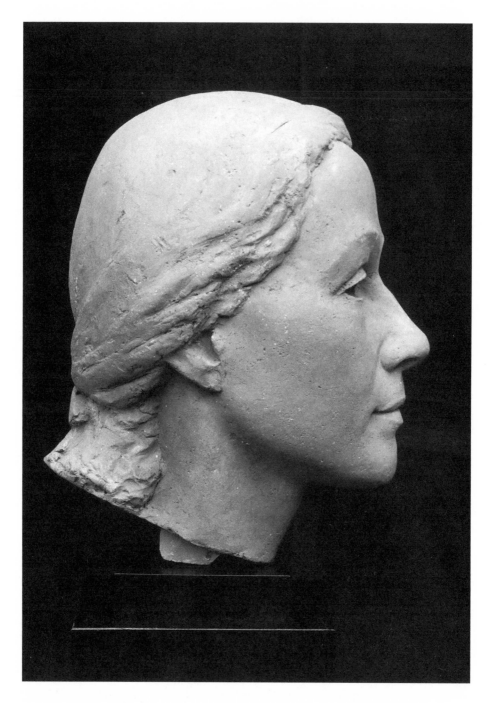

Portrait of Leslie, 1974, terra cotta on black painted base; profile view. Height: 17 ½ in. *Private Collection.*

Reclining Figure, 1959. Carved from Honduran mahogany depicting a female reclining on one elbow, nude, her head on her shoulder, legs bent at the knees. Dimensions: 12 x 30 in. *Private Collection.*

Above at left: *Bowl,* 1969, silver. Hammered, raised, and worked in repoussé. Marks: L.F. Dimensions: 1 x 3 ¾ in. (diam.) *Private Collection.*

Above at right: *Wine Tasting Cup,* 1964, silver hammered, raised, and worked in repoussé, grape leaf handle. Marks: L.F. Dimensions: 1 x 3 ½ in. (diam.) *Private Collection.*

Portrait of Leslie, 1960, terra cotta in the round; black painted base. Height: 17 ½ in.
Private Collection.

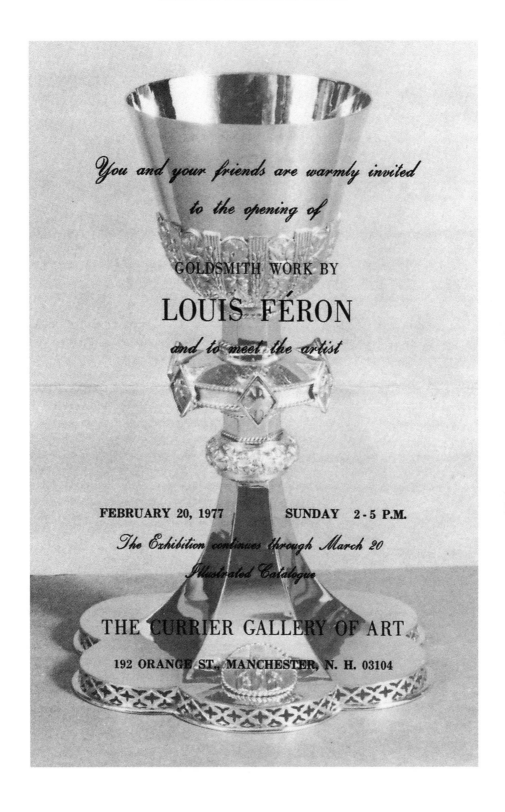

You and your friends are warmly invited

to the opening of

GOLDSMITH WORK BY

LOUIS FÉRON

and to meet the artist

FEBRUARY 20, 1977   SUNDAY   2-5 P.M.

The Exhibition continues through March 20

Illustrated Catalogue

THE CURRIER GALLERY OF ART

192 ORANGE ST., MANCHESTER, N. H. 03104

Strong Man, 1930, hammered bust in the round (seamless) from one sheet of half-red copper one meter square hammered over anvils. Made in a chaudronier workshop, Paris 1929-1930. Exhibited Salon d' Autonne, Le Petit Palais, Paris ca. 1930-1932. Lepine gold medal award for professional skill, 1932. Height: 26 in. *Collection of Mark Knowlton.*

Pectoral Cross, 1943, gold with precious stones. Height: 4 ½ in. *Collection Unknown.*

Head of an Indian Woman, 1949, carved mahogany in the round. Made in Costa Rica. Signed. Height: 20 in.

Unicorn, 1968, ivory with 22 kt. chased gold mane, tail, hooves horn and beard. Emerald eyes and emerald ornaments are set in the body. A diamond necklace is set in gold with an emerald drop. The silver base is chased with a floral design accented by gold dots. Designed also as an *objet d' art*, the unicorn can be removed from its base and worn as a clip. Marks: Louis Féron. Dimensions: 2 5/8 x 2 1/2".

Rouen Cathedral, Rouen, Normandy, France. Estel photo.

Chapter 5

Beginnings in Rouen

I was born in Normandy, France, in the city of Rouen on the sixteenth of August 1901 at Rue de la Cigogne du Mont. We were forty miles from the sea, less than a mile from the port on the Seine, and within walking distance of Rouen Cathedral. The Cathedral is near the central market and the church of St. Quen with its central radiant tower. Our neighborhood was that of the parish church of St. Vivien.

As far as I know, most of my relatives were born in or near Rouen. It is my belief that my earliest ancestors were from Denmark. My paternal grandfather was a sailor. I never knew him and I don't know his first name. I do remember seeing pieces of ivory and a shawl that he brought back from the Orient. He died at sea in his forties. He and his wife had two children, Ernest Nöel Féron, my father, and Aunt Eugénie, my father's younger sister.

Grandmother Féron later married a stepbrother of her first husband who was also a sailor. He drowned in the Seine, probably as a result of a fight. They had one son, Alexander. Alexander was a hearty man, full of life and joy and loved by our family. He adored my mother. When he was a small boy he was placed in an orphanage because Grandmother Féron became an alcoholic leading to her death. My mother took him out of the orphanage. She raised him until he was old enough to learn a trade, which happened to be glass blowing.

My maternal grandfather, Parisot, rescued a drowning child who had fallen off a barge into the Seine in the winter. His son, witnessing the fall from shore, exclaimed what he saw to his father who threw off some clothes and dove into the icy water. He found a little girl under the barge. On board, busy with bravos and congratulations, no one thought to give my grandfather dry clothes right away and he died of pneumonia a week later. He was in his early forties. I don't remember meeting him.

My Grandmother Parisot, who was blind from youth, lived with us after her husband died. She had a childhood friend, Anna, who lived with her for many years and was a nurse to my mother; consequently she came to live with the Férons too.

Anna never married. I understand that she had an affair in Paris and got caught as a victim in the repression of the insurrection, which broke out in Paris after the Franco-Prussian war. The location was Le Mur Des Fédérés. A man rounded up to be shot in front of the wall suddenly stood in front of Anna to shield her from gunshot. He was killed. Her shoulder was injured and it left one arm weak.

Anna truly earned the love of the Féron family. We all called her Grandmother Anna. She lived with us in Rouen and in Paris and moved to Rosny-Sur-Seine with my parents where she lived to be ninety-seven. She was deeply religious.

I had a cousin in Rouen. The sign outside his shop read: Féron, Férronnier. He made artistic works in iron—candelabra, iron grills, chairs, tables and ornaments. I also remember a tall attractive man who was a cousin of my mother. He was a Protestant with ancestry in Nüremberg, Germany, and lived near by. He was a carpenter of iron (*charpentier de fer*) and worked on ships, becoming known in Rouen as the one who climbed up the steeple of Rouen Cathedral to repair the copper rooster weather vane at the top. He was age forty at the time. There were six sons in his family, five of whom died in the First World War on the same ship, *Le Courbel*, which sank in the Dardanelles.

My father's uncle, Julien Varnier, who was my great-uncle, also lived near us. He was an aristocratic-looking man. I don't think he had a trade. He was bourgeois and well educated. He and his wife had no children. Uncle Julien provided money for my father's education in a Jesuit seminary, but fell upon hard times and the subsidy ended, and my father's education in the seminary was discontinued. It is my understanding that in their old age the Varniers moved to Rosny-Sur-Seine, where my parents took care of them.

Ernest Féron, my father, was a vigorous and jolly man. He loved to joke and tell stories and was rarely sad. Diligent and frugal, he earned his living as a journeyman in a textile mill working ten hours a day, six days a week. He had an affinity with the working man and was acutely aware of the hardships brought about by inferior working conditions and social injustice. Well-read and a good orator, he tried to organize a union. Although he was idealistic and optimistic, he could be strong-minded and authoritarian with a tendency to be impatient, impulsive and at times even violent. In the eyes of his employers, he was a troublemaker.

My mother, Louise Eugénie Parisot, was the daughter of a blind mother. She was dignified and quiet, but not gloomy. Like so many French women, she was overworked. She loved my father and stood by him, but considered him somewhat crazy to try to fight the losing battle of the poor. My mother was warmhearted and generous with an earthy wisdom. She had nine children, two of whom died at childbirth.

I was christened Louis Eugene Nöel Féron, and was the fourth or middle child, having four sisters and two brothers. My siblings were Ernestine, b. 1893; Jeanne, b. 1896; Julien, b. 1899; Albertine, b. 1903; Ernest, b. 1906; and Paulette, b. 1910. At birth, I weighed thirteen pounds, three ounces—my poor mother. Apparently, I made such a racket Grandmother Parisot said to her, "Twist his neck right away. He will give you trouble all your life." But shortly after, she asked to hold my head in her hands to study my face and said that she found me beautiful. At twelve months, I won first prize in a beauty contest with the promise that I would receive one hundred francs at age twenty-one. Being in military service in Alsace at the time, nothing came of it.

The earliest memory I have is taking a walk with Julien at about age two and a half. He led me out of the house to distance me from the spectacle of seeing Grandmother Parisot taken to the hospital where she later died. I remember the route we took passing a convent and a wall surmounted with a trellis dark in color. Before coming to the convent on the right, I saw a staircase. This staircase would take one to the road leading to the route to Darnétal.

Another early memory was Uncle Julien holding me in his arms during mass. I was looking intently at a man pulling out stops and using a foot pedal to pump air into the organ to make it play. Every Sunday I went to mass. This was at Saint-Vivien, our parish church, where I would eventually take my first communion. The music has stayed with me.

We drew our water from a Gothic fountain of stone that fascinated me called La Croix de Pierre. It was about three hundred meters down the hill from our house in the old section of Rouen. I was proud to help my mother by carrying water from the fountain in two buckets from a yoke on my shoulders. My sisters must have lugged the water up the stairs. I wore knickers and wooden soles on leather boots, and my father hammered nails on the bottom of the soles to extend their wear.

Our second home was a Norman-style, half-timbered house of wood and mortar built in the sixteenth century. It had three stories with small panes of glass in French windows that opened out. There were no sidewalks and the gutter ran down the center. Two large doors to the house opened onto a corridor where a small carriage would have been kept, if one had a carriage. At the end of the corridor to the right, there was a courtyard with chickens and an outhouse. To the left was a winding stone staircase, well worn, with two rooms off each of three landings. A cord from a ship was the railing, which seemed huge as a child. Julien and I shared one of the rooms on the top floor. It looked out onto a convent wall, and I still see and hear a heavy, creaking gate opening slowly from time to time and nuns disappearing into this mysterious place.

I remember a carved chestnut armoire with fruit ornaments, hand-made openwork hinges, forged door handles, and a large decorative key. There was a candleholder in twisted iron and on the wall a crucifix and a seashell with holy water (*de l'eau bénite*). An oil lamp of porcelain lit up the night when we were sick. It was something sacred for Julien and me. My two older sisters were in the other room, and the rest of the family shared two floors below. I recall a great long table with benches on either side and a coal stove where my mother prepared meals for all of us near a beautiful stone chimney.

I was sent to the municipal school, Michelet, like my brother who was there two years before me. Happy to learn and considered a good student by my schoolmasters, I was first in my class. I was also a fighter. My father checked the progress of our homework on his return from work. He helped to raise his children, to teach them and to do his share of the disciplining. I never saw him happier than when he was working with all of us. He was considerate with my mother, helping her in the home. At night, after a full day of work, he learned to mend clothes using the sewing machine and assisted her making shirts to augment family income. He repaired our shoes on Sundays. How could anyone not admire this man? Both of my parents would have lived one hundred years without their excessive burden of work.

A trait of my mother revealed itself. She said to my sister, "Go to find the midwife, I believe this baby is not going to wait." When the midwife arrived, my mother had given birth alone and was in the process of washing the sheets that had been soiled. It was cold. The midwife scolded her, but everything was in order. Several days later the baby died. No one cried.

I remember an infant in our neighborhood was not doing well. The doctor asked her if she was able to give milk. This poor little kid was so fearful. She took care of him until he regained his health.

When I was seven years old, our family moved to another section of Rouen called Mont Gargan. It was a mile or so from the opposite side of the Cathedral on the side of a hill named Côte Ste. Catherine. Here there were fields to play in. We had fruit trees and a little garden that I helped to take care of after doing my homework. There was a wonderful view across the valley. It was planted with apples and sometimes wheat where we would go to play, much to the anger of the proprietor who came to chase us on horseback. A man nearby thought this was dangerous and stopped him, holding the bridle of the horse. That was the end. We left.

I saw the beginning of aviation in Rouen. A neighbor, I think his name was Guilbeau, built an airplane of varnished wood and silk. It was elegant. My oldest sister worked sewing the silk on the wings. One fine day on Côte Ste. Catherine, pulled by an automobile, it rose up six or seven meters and then crashed—completely destroyed. Later this same man joined forces with the Norwegian explorer, Amundsen, during the research of the zeppelin. With my father and brother, I also remember seeing one of the first aviators, Morane, pass by onto the bridge across the city limits of Rouen. And at school, on the wall, there was a reproduction of Breguet flying over the Manche.

The flood in Rouen in 1910, the year of Halley's Comet, evoked my first big emotion. It was to see water almost submerge the city, water pouring frantically out of the mouths of sewers. Another alarming event was a cyclone right where we stood. Julien and I were taken by surprise returning from the Michelet school. We were near an iron gate. Julien ordered me to lie down and hold on to the gate. He did the same, saying, "Don't let go. Let's wait and see." We saw enormous plane trees uprooted and carried some hundred meters. A roof of a factory under construction was transported with the workers who were working on the top. It passed an arm of the Seine and landed with the men on Ile Lacroix without any loss of life. When we arrived home the family was relieved. And our house had been spared.

I have good reasons not to forget my small bed. One day, without my knowing it, my father saw me passing near a display of fruit. I stole an apple and quickly passed it to my brother. We were amused until we arrived in the house. My father was waiting red with anger. Immediately he took down our trousers and spanked us, I believe excessively. He ordered my mother to give us a piece of dry bread and send us to bed. I was suffering so much it was impossible to sleep and I was crying. Our mother came into the room alone and said, "Your father is right. I am sure you don't want to send him to jail, so learn your lesson. We must not steal. With stealing you will finish in the 'gallery' (an old expression). She kissed me good night, turning me on my side. We understood. But it's a fact; my bottom hurt me for a long time.

There were more rooms in this third home and an enormous fireplace and hearth large enough for benches where the entire family listened to my father read classics aloud. I was introduced to the writings of Moliére, Voltaire, Jean Jacque Rousseau, Victor Hugo and Diderot in this way, and a little later on to Anatole France, Alfred de Musset, George Sand and some poets. It is he who made me know certain American authors: Edgar Allan Poe, Jack London and James Fenimore Cooper. My father also sang. He adored the opera. He made a large puppet theater including scenery and puppets and put on little operas, taking all the parts and singing. It was great fun. The whole family enjoyed these *entertainments*. My father spoke good, correct French; I never heard him swear.

Every Sunday morning, my father, Julien and I walked from Mont Gargan to the central market near the place where Jeanne d'Arc was burnt. In winter, after making our purchases, my father stopped at a café and asked for *un petit sou*. This was a small glass of alcohol, I believe Calvados. He gave us just a taste. We brought back provisions and food in our bags and baskets. At home, food was simply prepared. We ate fish five days a week and meat on Sundays. There was an abundance of cream and butter. I never saw wine or alcohol at home. The Féron family drank from condensed milk cans, as there were no glasses. The rims of the cans were rounded.

My mother invariably set another place at the table for an unexpected guest. If she baked a pie or cake, the first slice was put on the windowsill as customary and picked up by a neighborhood child or someone less fortunate than we were. Guests were rarely invited to our house, but a beggar, or tradesman, a platelayer (*cheminot*) or a companion of duty (*compagnon du devoir*) traveling on foot to make his métier asking for water was never turned away. My mother asked him to come in, to sit down at our table and served him a meal. My father always made a cross on the bread before breaking it. Once I complained about the food on my plate. Without discussion, my dinner was promptly divided among the others. Our mealtime together was usually jolly. I remember a cheese that was so hard it wasn't edible. We started to joke about the cheese. It ended up as a game throwing it back and forth across the table and this made my mother unhappy.

One late afternoon, she said to me, "Louis, go along the route and greet your father. He looks strange." It was the twenty-fourth of December. I met him and he wished me a Merry Christmas without letting go of a sack that he carried over his shoulder. It was the first time I saw my father drunk. I had seen him at parties, happy and singing, drinking cider with friends, but this was different. His walking was not firm. When we arrived at the house, my mother, her face very tense, interrogated him with a look. Placing his heavy package on the floor he said, "It's Christmas."

"And your pay?" she asked.

He said, "I spent everything."

She began to cry and said, "How are we going to eat this week?"

I don't remember his exact words, in essence, "God will provide." My father was fed up not being able to give his family Christmas gifts. My mother never went against him openly; they had to settle things alone. It is true; we survived. It was the only Christmas our family had, and the most beautiful of rare Christmases that I have had in all my life. Other years we celebrated with several imported oranges flambée. Beside this one time, I don't remember having a toy; however, I loved playing with fire. My mother found it necessary to deliberately burn my finger on the stove to teach me to respect fire. When I complained, she burned it again, knowing that a deeper burn would hurt less. In my trade, I have seen an artisan do the same thing.

The memory of this brief period at Mont Gargan is joyful and dear to me. I went on foot crossing the valley passing by a property that was said to be haunted. I didn't believe it. Then I walked into the woods where I felt purified by the forest. I found a course of water that I still dream about and took off my shoes and walked around in this beautiful clear stream full of little pebbles. Continuing to the source there was a whispering river.

I had been sent to pick up bread at the baker, six pounds, three kilograms, as usual. It was rare that the weight was exact. The baker cut what was called *la pesée* to adjust the weight. I usually ate this on my return up the hill. I remember that Ernestine, my eldest sister, in charge when my mother was absent, would ask, "Where is the *pesée*," knowing well what happened to it. Also, she had seen me playing in the river. She had good eyesight. Something else I remember was the manner of counting up purchases. The baker took a stick and cut it in two. One was for the customer and one for the baker. He then joined the two sticks together and marked the purchases on both, remitting one to the customer. When payment day arrived the sticks were matched, avoiding errors.

Another time, Julien and I were sent to pick up bread and, arriving at the haunted property, I asked him to make the short ladder in order to see over the wall that surrounded the estate. He offered his two hands together for my foot; thus I was able to arrive at the top to look on the other side. Julien asked what I was seeing, but I was too busy looking to answer him. There was a beautiful pond and a boat half sunk in a swamp. Everything was so green and quiet. I felt happy, but Julien not at all. More than fifty years later, I went back to look again. During the war the English made their quarters in Rouen and transformed this site into a hospital, clean, repaired and superb. I was a little disappointed.

One dry summer, the rains had not filled the cistern that normally provided us with water. I went to a spring near our house. Waiting my turn, a young girl observed some holes in my socks that she called potatoes. The color of my skin in contrast to my socks made her think of potatoes. My anger would ordinarily have led me to jump on her. Vexed and ashamed of being insulted I felt like a coward. I had been educated not to fight with a girl or woman. She was sixteen or seventeen. I took my buckets full of water and cried on the path to the house.

When Jeanne learned what happened, she went down with me to the spring and asked, "Which one?"

I answered, "That one."

The young girl, astonished, received a good smack from Jeanne who said to her, "That is for the potatoes."

I stopped crying, having received vengeance, but afterwards it bothered me. I felt sorry for the girl. My mother made it clear that a man must be courageous in all sorts of defense, to help women and not to cry; also my oldest sister was always ready to fix my clothes that I often brought back torn and I would receive a smack: all of this succeeded in making me incapable of not pardoning women. I prefer to be the loser.

I was by far the most active and naughtiest child in our family, earning beatings from my father and daily slaps from my mother. If I did nothing wrong, she would say, "That is for the time I missed you." I loved to explore and get lost for the day, following soldiers to a field where they carried out maneuvers. Attracted by sailing boats, I disappeared to the port on the Seine. Everybody was looking for me. There was a fear of water in my family, inborn perhaps in Normans. On my return, naturally I was punished. Once I converted my mother's kitchen knives into little saws and used my father's woodworking tools to dig out chunks of limestone from a bank near the house. I dragged the stones home on an improvised sled and went to work on my first carvings. He kept these early pieces, but I don't think he ever completely forgave me for destroying his woodworking tools.

My father walked with Julien and me, pointing out Rouen's architecture, windows and carvings in wood and stone. He made us notice street lanterns, a decorative grill or gate, a doorknocker, locks and door mounts. Some of my first impressions of beauty were through him. We visited Rouen Cathedral, the abbey of St. Quen and other churches and museums together. It is remarkable to think of the love this man had for religious art in spite of his disapproval of priests.

The road behind our house led to the Bonsecours Chapel for sailors where there were certain small replicas of ships that the Virgin had saved. I still dream about them.

On a summer evening, my father, Uncle Alexander, Julien and I went to see the circus where a wrestler offered a few francs to someone who could push him to the ground. It was enough to tempt my uncle, who loved sports, and was a so-called Master of Arms from military service, whatever that means. He handed his things to my father and sent the wrestler to the ground twice. The public applauded; then the circus gave the promised sum of money to my uncle. As we were leaving, we hadn't gone ten steps, when four men incited my uncle and my father, neither of whom were intimidated. Alexander said to my father, "Take the kids. I'm going to fix this." My father refused to leave. Alexander backed himself up against the wall and with his feet and fists punched two of them out of the fight. One was still there. He threw him to the ground. The fourth retired from altercation. Taking no chances my uncle said, "Now we must run. He is waiting for others to come." There ends the story.

Once we went on an excursion to a family picnic in a carriage with wooden benches called a *char-à-bancs*. Alexander did the cooking for all of us. His wife was a peasant from Picardy and they had two girls. The last time I saw him, I was thirteen years old. He showed me a beeswax roll with an early musical recording on it that he played, and an experiment that produced an electric shock. Alexander disappeared in World War I. My father searched for years looking for him without success.

I admired Julien but never played with him because he was too quiet and serious and didn't like to fight. Next to my father, he was the most intelligent member of the family. He was an excellent draftsman with an interest in mechanics and became an engineer and finally a director in a laboratory of an aeronautics factory. My father was extremely proud of him. Julien often won prizes at school. Once, there were so many he needed help to carry them off the platform. In France, it was customary to make a holiday out of a certain day in July to reward the outstanding students in each town. The notables, parents and children came to the town hall or central meeting place and the mayor presided. No one worked that day. Red-covered books and wreaths were distributed to the winners and the ceremony was celebrated with a feast. Julien and I won prizes every year. The only books that I owned in my youth were prizes from school. Every one of my teachers pressured me to keep up with Julien. It was annoying.

At the end of a school year, a classmate of Julien attacked him, not realizing my presence. Why he did this, I never knew, for Julien was peaceable. Abandoning my books and jumping on him like a wild animal, biting and pulling his hair and kicking with my feet, he wasn't able to get free of me and pleaded with Julien for help. I think Julien almost took the position of his classmate. Returning home I wasn't punished, but I wasn't congratulated either.

Prior to the celebration of one thousand years of Normans in Rouen, the explorer, doctor and oceanographer, Jean Baptiste Charcot came in his sailing ship, the *Pourqoi Pas?* He had returned from the South Pole in June of 1910 to have his vessel repaired, to give speeches and to hold a reception for the authorities. The two best students from each school in Rouen were invited on board with their parents. Julien and I were chosen and our parents accompanied us. Admiral Charcot shook hands with everyone. I saw the sea for the first time and tasted my first sip of wine. It was from a barrel using a siphon like a genuine sailor. The ship was a beauty. It was a great day.

Easter of 1911, my father moved his family to Paris. His decision has a turbulent history. The famous Dreyfus case had a retrial in Rennes in the early 1900s after a violent campaign of revision that lasted two years, 1897–1899. The affair divided France into two camps, cutting through all classes. My father took a strong position in favor of Dreyfus. Rouen was predominantly Catholic and conservative. The official position was against the release of Dreyfus, who was a French army captain accused and condemned to die for espionage in 1894. This so infuriated my father he became anti-priest thereafter. In my father's opinion, Alfred Dreyfus, an Alsatian Jew, had been framed. He felt that the Catholic Church should recognize the facts of the case or they were not practicing the Christian faith. Dreyfus was pardoned and rehabilitated in 1906 by a judgment of the court.

Because of his views, my father lost his job in the mill. Although he found work elsewhere, it was for less pay, and over the next several years it became clear that he would never advance in Rouen. He needed better employment to feed his large family and was forced to sell most of his possessions. He lived his life by a moral code and impressed upon his children the importance of having a clear conscience and a clean name.

I don't think any of us realized what we would lose by leaving Rouen. We thought we were part of Rouen for life. The fact of living so much on the edge and so close together physically, a unity of flesh, almost animal, brought a joy and warmth. All of life consisted of taking care of someone else. I have experienced that.

Chapter 6

Paris

Aunt Eugénie, my father's sister, was married to a house painter, Victor Massot, who was a quiet gentleperson. The two men got along well except on the subject of politics. My father, a Christian Socialist, accused Uncle Victor of nourishing anarchistic ideas. The Massots had moved from Rouen to Paris a few years earlier and offered to house our family until we found an apartment.

The Massots adopted a young girl whose father was killed in a strike in Brittany. An incident in Rouen comes to mind. As a child I was unjustly accused of biting into a pear that wasn't ripe. Many years later she confessed that she was the one who bit into the pear. My mother turned to her husband and said, "You see, I told you that Louis would never lie."

First jobs were secured for Ernestine, who was eighteen, and Jeanne, who was fifteen. The two girls and Julien took the train to Paris. Albertine, Ernest and Paulette followed. Anna lived in a nursing home until we were settled, and I stayed with my parents to help with the move. What anguish to see our furnishings leave. The oven where Julien had hidden some money was sold, too, and the armoires and our crucifix, all of it gone. Then the day arrived. We closed up and left Normandy for the unknown.

I was desperate with this sudden imprisonment in a city apartment and terribly homesick for Rouen. My aunt was an angel, a simple and good woman. She tried to comfort me by asking what she could do to make me feel better. Mixing up a flour paste with newsprint, I made some mountains using table salt for snow. I had never seen a real mountain. After that, she took me out into the locality.

The neighborhood was called Ménilmontant in *arrondissement* XX. My father found a job in a factory that made precision gauges and became foreman. Ménilmontant was an interesting place, principally inhabited by artisans. It was an underprivileged area, but not a slum. I have vivid memories of a highly successful socialistic cooperative there called "a Bellevilloise." It was created to provide the highest quality at the lowest price and was open to everyone. The profits were returned to the participants and customers who enjoyed the services it provided. They included; a pharmacy, a clinic, a dispensary, stores for food and clothing, provisions (such as coal), a gymnasium, a brasserie with a billiard table, a theater for music, even a small symphony orchestra, night classes, lectures, meetings and a summer camp. Profits were actually used to improve the community. It worked as an honest, uncorrupted cooperative until 1918, about forty years. Without it, I don't know what our family would have done. Then, the fight between the socialists and communists started. The communists took over, stole the profits, swiped the priceless library of artisan books, demoralized the people, and ruined the cooperative.

My father led Julien and me to Rue des Amandiers. This is a narrow street almost parallel to Rue Sorbier where our school was located. It was lined with bistros. He showed us the deprivation of people drinking absinthe and how degrading it was for working people. We saw men slumped over tables looking stupefied and idiotic. He explained that asylums were filled with victims. It was horrible. Later, I heard it rumored that the French government had made absinthe cheaply available to the working class after France's defeat in the Franco-Prussian war and the bloody revolution that followed in Paris in 1871. The French government killed more than twenty thousand Parisians. With the start of World War I, absinthe was quickly suppressed.

I went to the municipal school for boys on Rue Sorbier. The kids tried to insult me by calling me peasant in their pretension to be pure Parisian. I was not one who refused a fight. Ripping off my belt and snapping it, I answered, "I'm not a peasant; I'm a pirate." With this nicely understood, I was respected and happy in my new school. I believe the reason I loved school right away was the presence of a sculpture in stone above the front entrance. My dreams from boyhood in Normandy came to mind and what I saw was interpreted as a good sign for my future as a sculptor.

Working from antique plasters, I received my first lessons in drawing that were part of the basic training. Once a week there were workshops in metal and wood. The professors of these workshops are the only ones I remember well in the school. One of them later recommended that I go to evening classes. I suppose my parents were happy to get rid of me. Here there was modeling, anatomy with live models and sculpture. The professor was outstanding. I was the only child present. This continued for four years until I was old enough to be admitted to L'École Municipal d'Art de Belleville.

Having skipped a grade, I completed my course at Rue Sorbier before age thirteen. By law I was too young to receive my primary school certificate. Three scholarships to study art were offered to me. It was agreed that I go to Germain Pelon Art School as a scholarship student from the City of Paris, but World War I started in France on August 3, 1914. The art schools closed, the teachers went to war, and the workshops shut down. Suffering was for everyone. The famous canon, Big Bertha, sent shells over Paris every five minutes. Everything was upset. There was no other solution for my education. I was sent back to Rue Sorbier to repeat my last year again and again. Fortunately, an attentive professor gave me advanced studies in mathematics and science. I learned to study alone.

After school I was restless and got into many street fights. My father recognized that I needed to fight and arranged for a family friend to give me boxing lessons in the gym at Belleville. I became so good at it I was a menace in the neighborhood. They called me, Louis Féroce—the ferocious. Two more attempts were made to channel my explosive energy: violin lessons with an Alsatian teacher and singing lessons, both of which failed.

At fourteen, I met a beautiful lyric actress and musician with red hair. She was twenty-five, married with two children and lived at Place Des Fêtes. She had confidence in me and encouraged my studies at L'École Belleville where she had a scholarship. I felt that she was looking for affection. Our friendship lasted for some time. She told me that men who are initiated by prostitutes become rotten. "I don't want that for you, Louis." One evening when I met her at the theater after the show she said, "I can't see you tonight," and she sent me home. Another day she said, "You must understand I can't live in this apartment and buy my clothes and food without money. My friends help me; I have never asked you for money." I didn't listen any more. I was wounded. Later on I learned that a wealthy furrier kept her. My father, who reproached me for having an affair with a married woman, happened to run into her on the street. She inquired about me. My father came near, looked into my eyes and asked, "What should I answer?" I replied, "Don't count on me." I remained aloof for two years or more.

There was only one young woman I tolerated among the youth I grew up with at Rue Boyer. A group of us took walks on Sundays. At this time, she did not represent the same image of deception. Marguerite's parents had an apartment at the corner of our street. Her father was a mechanic of precision instruments for optometry. There were four children. Her mother, a mother hen, one day lied to the police to protect me as I had just broken a window while playing. "No, it was not *petit* Louis," she said. "I saw the kid run away." Closing her eyes on my relationships she made up her mind that I was going to marry her daughter.

In our neighborhood a younger boy showed me a tattoo he had just received with three dots between the thumb and forefinger on his left hand. I told him that this tattoo was given to a member of a gang or anti-social person and that later it could prevent him from getting work. It could even ruin him. He was noticeably upset. I proposed removing it. He agreed. I sharpened my knife and he gritted his teeth. Drawing a lot of blood, I scraped and scraped until I removed the marks. He was brave. Neither of us thought about the possibility of infection. Many years later I met him on the street with his wife. He said to her, "Here is the man who saved my life."

The war continued. I made a 350-kilometer bicycle ride in one day to say goodbye to Julien before he went to the front. He survived the war but was killed in a bombardment in World War II at age forty-two. He was married with no children.

My father's salary was frozen during the war, and obviously there was no money for my education. When I was fourteen and some months, he told me that I should leave school and learn a trade. An inventor who was an acquaintance of my father accepted me as an apprentice. After three weeks or so, disinterested with the work, I surprised him by carving with his materials, on his time, three small hammers, each about three quarters of an inch long. He sent me out but beforehand gave me very good advice, "Louis, go to the town hall of *arrondissement* XL. On the bulletin board you will see some notices by artisans offering to take apprentices." As I was leaving, he added "Maybe you will be an artist, but never a mechanic." Now that is not altogether true.

At this moment, my beautiful life started. I went to the town hall and discovered that a chaser (*ciseleur*) by the name of Volk was looking for an apprentice to retouch bronze castings for editions of sculpture. I visited his workshop and saw sculptures in bronze which were being repaired and refined from the castings. The atmosphere was artistic and pleasant under the direction of Monsieur Jean Volk, who became my master. His father and grandfather had been chasers in bronze (*ciseleurs en bronze*) and trained in guild traditions. He asked me if I was good in drawing, anatomy and modeling, encouraging me to take night classes, and I reassured him.

My mother came with me to the Volk's workshop on Rue Popincourt, in a neighborhood of bronze trades near Boulevard Voltaire. It was in a courtyard. Around the courtyard were artisan workshops and each worked in metal. It was customary for the owner to live with his family in adjoining rooms. Monsieur Volk did not ask where my father was. During the war, men of my father's age were at the front if they were physically fit or in the army somewhere. Having seven children and being a mechanic, it was more useful from the government's point of view to keep him in his workshop. Also, my mother was somewhat afraid of my father's temper. It was with this reasoning that she was willing to lie by omission and sign the contract that was normally signed by the father. Back home my mother explained that I was now in a place where I would be happy. My father visited the Louvre and other museums with me Sundays and encouraged my desire to be an artist and so he was pleased. Once a week I received just enough money to pay for the bus. I saved this money and ran to work from our apartment, exhilarated, and eager to arrive one quarter of an hour before the other artisans.

After that, thanks to Jean Volk, my life took the direction that was never to change in my lifetime; the love of my trade, the pride to be a sculptor-orfèvre, the pleasure to excel in it, and the ability to insure my life as a free man. Volk cured me of my complexes from childhood to be too small and poor. Almost immediately he treated me as an adopted son. Every morning he was receiving breakfast at his bench. He said that he didn't like to have breakfast alone. My place was to his left. His wife always brought the same for me. Both knew that we were missing money at home and that I was undernourished. This attention continued until I left Volk and he never alluded to it. Madame Alice Volk and her husband were interested in taking care of me exactly as parents. They had one girl, Janet, and no boys. They trusted me, which I believe made them dream that when I returned from the army, maybe I would be able to marry Janet and be the successor to Volk's business, the complete workshop, which he received from his own master.

By 1916, chasing a cast (*ciseleur en fondue*) had long since become a separate trade. It is a small part of the *art of chasing*, encompassing elaborate techniques that master gold and silversmiths have used for thousands of years to shape and embellish metal with hammer and chisel. An artisan in Volk's workshop was called a *figurist* and chased bronze sculptures only. When I arrived at this workshop there was only one master, Dieudome, who was lame and not eligible for the war, five companions and one other apprentice.

My workweek was seventy-two and three quarter hours, including one hour for lunch, 6:45 a.m. to 7:00 p.m. weekdays and to 7:30 p.m. on Saturdays. I was given a traditional blouse to wear. After doing chores, I learned how to make tools and how to use them. Although he was not a master himself, Monsieur Jean had a thorough understanding of the trade and a great gift in transmitting his knowledge. He was strict and maintained a high level of craftsmanship. One of the first pieces I chased was a replica of *Lion of the Tuileries*, a bronze sculpture by the nineteenth century French artist, Barye. As an apprentice, I enjoyed going to the foundry to pick up newly cast sculptures for the workshop. Seeing the flaming crucible and the pouring of metal into investment molds captivated me. Eight years later I worked for six months in a bronze foundry.

Every Saturday evening Volk made an inspection of the shop. If the assigned work was done, I received a tip that was enough for my mother to buy my food. One time, roughhousing with the other apprentice, I smashed some plaster statuary off a shelf and lost my tip.

One day, Monsieur Jean called me into his office and said, "I have something for your mother, Louis." He took the four-year contract and tore it up in pieces saying," Give this to her. Monday, you will start as a companion and we will see how much you can earn." I had been an apprentice for two years, instead of the four that was customary. The next week I was able to bring to my mother what I had earned in sixty hours of work. Her first idea was to take me to the tailor to have a blue suit made to order. I was so proud because afterwards, when I went out on Sunday, my friends knew that I was a companion.

Everything was going well. I was now seventeen and earning slightly more than my father was. Feeling that he understood me, Monsieur Volk asked if I was willing to promise to marry Janet, who was less than fourteen years old, and that he would give me the workshop if I kept my word. He did not know that I was already involved in affairs with women. It was a turning point, a point of no return. I could not agree to his plan. He said under those circumstances we could not work together any more. I accepted the customary eight-day notice. On the eighth day he tried to avoid the issue, but I stopped him at the door asking for my money. He gave it to me regretfully. We were both mad, and I was forgetting his goodness. At this moment my life with Volk stopped, but I still keep my affection for him and for his wife. I soon realized how exact and important his teachings were and how fortunate I was. The disciplines learned with Volk permitted me to work with great assurance and speed. Bronze is more resistant and difficult to chase than precious metal. It develops a sure and steady hand.

We saw each other afterwards. It happened in the same neighborhood where I was working with Delsinne. I met Volk in the street and was glad to see him again. It was 1933, and I had won the title of Best Worker of France (Meilleur Ouvrier de France) as best chaser of France, had been named Commander of the Order of Work (Commandeur du Ordre du Travail) and was decorated in the Sorbonne by the French government. I asked Volk if he knew about my nomination. He said, "Yes, but you are still my apprentice."

To finish this important period in my life, I must report an experience in a New York restaurant, Le Gourmet, managed by the former auto racer, Dryfus. I believe it was 1946 or 1947. We were seated at the table telling jokes, all of us French and from or associated with the same trade. One joke left me feeling sad.

Being the only one who didn't laugh, Simon Barens, looked at me and said, "Oh, we forgot you are not a Jew." There was a pause, and then he asked. "Tell me Louis, where did you learn the trade?"

"In Paris," I replied.

"But where?" he asked, and I answered, "32 Rue Popincourt," Again there was a pause.

"The name of your master?"

"Volk," I answered.

"Ah, a Jew—so you have been educated by a Jew in the ghetto."

This was a revelation to me and explains why Volk was so mad. His anger wasn't coming from the fact that I was unwilling to marry his daughter. He believed that I refused his offer to receive his workshop because he was Jewish. This is something I was not able to conceive of at the time, being educated by a family without prejudice. I was sincere. Living by principles was ingrained in me. I never thought about differences between people other than a natural sympathy or the reverse. My father left Rouen as a result of being a Dreyfusard. He was born into a Catholic family. To be a Dreyfusard for a Catholic was like treason. For me, it was the beginning of very good luck. I received, thanks to this transfer, a wider education and an opportunity to learn the trade that gave me assurance in this life.

The turmoil continued. I was hungry to learn and in rebellion against the war that seemed endless. At home tensions were mounting. My father was remonstrating about my family dependence, my age, my salary, and that I was a companion. In a rage over some remark that I stupidly made, he threw something at my head from the table, which caused a slight wound. My mother saw the blood and panicked. They went into the bedroom common to all of us. After a while she returned to the table where everyone was amazed. Without sitting down my mother said to me, "Go and apologize to your father, you have been wrong." I did so. My father was in tears. He took me in his arms and kissed me. We calmed down. He said to me, "It is not what you said that saddened me, it is the first time I have argued with your mother." It's true she had taken something from the table ready to defend me. I am unable to talk about this dispute without crying. They were so good and adorable, both of them. While reading these memoirs to Leslie, she consoled me saying that it was good for me to cry, even at ninety-six years of age. I did all that was necessary to be pardoned, but—

A job presented itself in a bronze figure workshop near Place de la Republique owned by Lecouty who used to be a very good chaser. As a matter of fact, he had a piece in Musée Des Fabricants de Bronze d'Art. He was a good businessman. There were three masters, twenty-seven companions and no apprentices, but the quality of the chasing, in spite of Lecouty's fame, was far below Volk's standards. I was hired as a companion. The salary was higher and the sculptures I worked on were by more interesting sculptors—Rodin and Bourdelle, for example. I worked there for more than one year.

At Place Gambetta I saw a fight between German and French aircraft. Tracer bullets in the night sky gave the illusion of fairyland enchantment where death played out. I saw an enormous bomb fall from a zeppelin at Rue Ménilmontant, cutting in two a building of five or six floors. This was seventy-five meters from our house. As I was coming out of the movies, the alert sounded and the movie public emptied into the street. Running up Rue Ménilmontant, I was stopped by the police who had just arrived. I tried to advance, being only fifty steps from Rue Boyer, but was blocked by the fire. The firemen were fighting to save victims. A tense policeman gave me a whack. Running, I retraced my steps, taking Rue Sorbier and by this detour I arrived at our house. It was intact. Then, at the corner a bomb fell but did not explode. Soldiers disarmed it the next morning and the people applauded these brave men. If it had exploded, I wouldn't be writing this. As I recall, six or seven zeppelins had been sent to bomb the poor neighborhoods of Paris. Fleeing, they let go of all of their bombs and only one returned to its base.

Chapter 7

Les Indélicats

In 1919, I left home abruptly following a disagreement with my father. He started to roll up his sleeves the way he did when I was a child. I did the same. My mother touched me on the shoulder saying, "Nobody should fight with his own father. The door is not nailed." I took my jacket and departed without a penny in my pocket and did not return for eight years. I adored my parents and still do today. My father was filled with idealism and joy of life. He was always ready to learn and took pleasure in teaching. My mother was courageous and generous. She had good common sense. I never forgot her proverbs and her affection, but the umbilical cord was cut. Two of my four sisters, Ernestine and Jeanne, were married. Julien was in the army. Three of my siblings still lived at home, but all of our lives were transformed and the close family bond that we had enjoyed was broken.

Marguerite's sister loaned me fifty francs and I rented a small room at a hotel. This was a solitary period living alone. Going to the library, I devoured classics, philosophy and science and often read walking to the job, missing my father and Volk, both of whom used to guide me. Every evening I went to L'École d'Art Belleville. Coming back late to my hotel, sometimes I played pool in the café with the proprietor to unwind before retiring. I was mixing with different groups of people with the hope to learn what life did not permit me to learn. At times I may have been in bad company, but I always worked toward the accomplishment of my dream as a child to become a sculptor.

A sculpture professor came to Belleville in 1923 by the name of Julius Cladel. He was the brother of Judith Cladel, a biographer and one of the many women attached to Rodin. She was credited with having urged him to marry Rose, his faithful companion and servant. I developed a long friendship with Julius that lasted until my departure from France in 1934. In a general competition in Paris (1926) I received third prize for sculpture. There were about eight hundred competitors. Julius took notice and would have been happy to see me working with him, but there was a very important reason why I did not accept and could not tell him. I had no money and was unwilling to go through more deprivation in order to study with him.

I had known from my arrival in Paris in 1911 what I would call misery. There were ten of us living in three rooms without running water and one toilet for two floors of families. The apartment was without sun. To find a decent apartment for a family often was impossible with our means. I needed to fold up my bed early every morning so that my mother could open the drawer to take out the dishes to make breakfast. Bathing was done in a municipal facility. There was hunger and cold and my one pair of shoes took in water and snow in spite of the newspapers I stuffed into them. I stood in line with tickets for food and coal that were in short supply and rationed. I don't accuse anyone, even less my parents, because they were perfect as parents, and I remember that even with hardships we were not a sad family. But the fact remained; I was under the obligation to earn my living early, which deprived me of the leisure necessary to the development of an artist. My friend, Pierre Bourdelle, whom I met in New York in 1945, told me once that an artist needs to spoil two years of his life with the leisure to dream.

Everything I have been able to learn beside my trade has been taken from sleeping hours. Secretly I laugh thinking of this time when I was asking God not to leave me without work. My prayer was answered;

I never stopped working! I was full of confidence and trusted my intelligence, paying attention to keep my health, convinced that good luck will come, and when good luck comes, I must be ready and worthy. I listened to old teachers, knowing that what I needed to learn in this period was only available from highly experienced craftsmen.

Six months before leaving for the army, there was a slight set back in Lecouty's workshop. Being the youngest and the most recent companion, I expected to be laid off. I heard about the neighborhood of Saint Antoine where the furniture industry is located. It is near Place de la Bastille where the French Revolution started in 1789. A chaser named Opel was looking for a companion chaser who was also a figurist. Here I learned ornament chasing that I was lacking and happy to add to my knowledge.

In January 1921, I took the train for Épinal, where I was called to military service. My mother and Marguerite came to *La Gare L'EST* to say goodbye. While kissing me, my mother pressed several bills of francs into my hand. I was surprised to see her as I was completely without news of my family. She must have learned about my departure through Marguerite. She came alone without my father, perhaps secretly.

I was in the army for two years; a sad experience. After the first examinations, the chiefs decided that I had a better education than the other recruits did. They put me into the group to be trained as brigadiers. Problems followed as a result of this. I have never liked exercising authority or suffering from it. Quickly, it was decided that I would be better as secretary to the colonel, who was the commander of the battalion, and later on someone capable of organizing the store of clothing, which was in disorder as a result of the war. The clothes were torn and full of blood. After several months, everything was cleaned and repaired. I submitted an inventory and the army officials were pleased. Then the kitchen, in a terrible state, was given to me to correct. Before this assignment and for more than one year, I had suffered from a poor diet, poorly prepared. There was not enough food. Marguerite sent me small amounts of money from my savings and I tried to supplement the mess hall by buying sardines and chocolate. But now I was reorganizing the kitchen and things were better for me. I arranged to get fresh fish from the seashore and went daily to the slaughterhouse to buy meat.

I understand that inadequate nourishment in my youth and military service was responsible for my small stature and the state of my teeth. I was twenty-five or six before I had enough money to go to the dentist for the first time and was tormented with bad teeth like many Frenchmen of my class. In the late 1970s during my first hospitalization for an operation, old tuberculosis scars appeared in the X-rays.

The army provided free tobacco. One had to sign if he did not want tobacco. I tried smoking a cigarette once at Volk's that made me feel sick. In the army I learned to tolerate tobacco, and smoked a pipe to free my hands. In the 1950s in New York, a man died in my studio from tobacco addiction. I stopped smoking immediately, but after thirty years of smoking, the damage to my nervous system and to my teeth was permanent.

One day, a superior asked me to punish a cook. I didn't believe he was guilty and I refused to discipline him. This superior got mad and threatened me. I felt that he was preparing a kind of trap. Thus, in the morning I went to the infirmary declaring myself sick. I was not shaved; I was dirty, depressed and fuming. The male nurse, to whom I told my story, put me in a corner. When the doctor arrived, he asked what was wrong with the brigadier.

The nurse answered, "Oh, he has a very red throat, a slight fever and his appearance is poor."

Without any examination and without hesitation, they sent me to the military hospital. In the army there is always the terror of contagion. I left with sick people on a bus and was received by a sister of the contagious ward. She gave me an injection against diphtheria and this made me sick for one day. I was, however, obliged to stay in the ward for the twenty or twenty-one day quarantine.

I started to draw the other patients. Everything was quiet. Nobody noticed that the doctor was watching me. He asked me to come to his laboratory and asked that I help him because he was not drawing well and there was no camera equipment at his disposal. Encouraged, I started the next morning with a new job. Besides drawing, I was copying his research, looking into the microscope and learned to use all the apparatus. Really, for three months, I was living like a king, but the army forced him to decide either to discharge me from the army or to give me three months convalescence pay. If the army discharged me, they would have to give me a pension, which they obviously did not want to occur. The latter was done.

The question was where was I to live in Paris? Marguerite rented an apartment, but I felt that I had to get married, being too proud to return to my parents. As a result, we got married. I was less than twenty-one years of age. During these three months, Volk offered me work that I gratefully accepted. I was counting on the salary and remitted it to Marguerite, who then sent me money during the rest of my military duty. With the occupation of the Ruhr, I had to serve three extra months.

After military service, I wanted to finish my education related to my trade. I had in mind to return to L'École d'Art Belleville in the evenings with friends of my youth and to visit the museum of L'Académie Montparnass. I worked hard to protect our life and was routinely at my bench by 7:30 am. The times had changed and we were doing a forty-eight hour week instead of sixty or seventy-two. I was enjoying more time, permitting me to study and sculpt and my marriage suffered as a result of these activities. It seemed to me that if I was able to inspire confidence in Marguerite, eventually we would be more at ease and proud to achieve what appeared to be an impossibility for a man of my background.

One evening, the new director of the school, trying to regain discipline after the war, required a late student to produce a paper with an excuse from his parents. This caused a rebellion among a group of about fifteen men. We decided to leave the school and to meet every Thursday in a café near *metro* Oberkampf. The custom to see one another once a week continued for me until I left France for Costa Rica in 1934. We exchanged ideas and critiques of our works: paintings, sculpture, engravings, movies, and all of our projects related to art.

At the same time we were observing French political life and were slowly able to feel what was coming, whether fascism or communism. I suspected that these two political convictions had something in common. Namely, they obliged people by force to obey the convictions of the party. If you were neither communist nor fascist, you were accused of being anarchist. The communists practiced infiltration (*noyautage*), profiting from the law of the majority. While the life of the worker improved, the communists appeared in all the works everywhere and destroyed everything. I saw it happening.

I remember a battle in front of our doorway between six or seven communists and me, who they knew as the "enemy." They insulted me. After handing my raincoat to a friend, I crossed the street. The one who insulted me apologized, while one from behind hit me and grabbed me by my long hair. On the ground, a mêlée began. I was able to stand on his shoulders. My feet hit two of the communists. Once again I jumped on one of them and seized him by the neck under my arm. My father arrived and began to help me by pushing them away. The two of us went to the tobacco store nearby. The people at the window had seen everything. Suddenly my father realized that one of the men was bleeding from the eye and left to go and see what I had done. "Stay here," he said, "You can ruin your life with a thing like this." After some time he came back and reported that it was not serious, but his eyelid was torn. "How did you wound him so badly?" he asked. I had a nest of pencils in my pocket as always and one of them must have hit his eyelid. My father sent me up to the house, grumbling about my *mauvais* (evil) obsession to fight back. He warned me that I would be scorned, but behind his words there was a growing hatred for both the communists and the socialists. In the future, I avoided going to socialist reunions and the Syndicate Orfèvrerie. Later, I met the same vile person. Marguerite was with me. I gave her my packages, but he refused to fight. He was alone.

After the liberation, during a demonstration at Place de l'Opéra for the forty-eight hour week, I saw a police officer, without provocation, shoot and kill a young man standing near me. In 1927, I observed an enormous memorial on Champs Elysées for Sacco and Vanzetti. This demonstration remained peaceful.

As I had a habit of reading while walking to work, I took the shortest route across the cemetery called Père Lachaise, where it is said that only the great names are buried. I witnessed a brutal uprising nearby at the Mur des Fédérés. A well-dressed man questioned the police officer regarding the manners of his men. The officer noted how the questioner was dressed and answered, "Where do you think we recruit these men, from the university?" Because of these events and to this day, I am uncomfortable in crowds, even in church.

The artists I have referred to call themselves *Les Indélicats* (The Indelicates). Lérouille, one of the artists, initiated the name. After a fiery discussion, it was accepted reluctantly. Maybe it was the truth. I don't know who proposed publishing a *cahier* in which every member would be represented with a linoleum print. After exchanging ideas, a theme was chosen for a particular issue in protest of what we were witnessing in French society. Unfortunately my set of *cahiers* disappeared or became lost in my travels. I would say that the tendency of the group was individualistic, not anarchist. I shall try to remember each of these men.

Lérouille was a painter and a musician who we called *La baleine*, the whale. The war interrupted his art training in 1914, but he returned to our Belleville school. For us he was already an old man. He was the creator of a school of painting called musicalist, continuing in the style of the impressionists, which was no longer popular in France. He worked as a mechanic to escape being a slave of the galleries. I found him to be honest and sensible and he was one of my best friends. He won the prize money for the song of Les Indélicats paid for by Debardieux, and at the café immediately consumed it in drinks. He had been teaching Robin the métier of painting, giving him the house, the table, and guiding him during his career without receiving any gratitude from Robin. Lérouille was a grand monsieur.

Debardieux was a painter and the most intellectual of the gang. He was a remarkable draftsman and the one responsible for shaping the painter, Maurice Estève. Debardieux was from a well-to-do family. His father was a publisher of books for the army. He too was a good friend. Estève developed ideas received from Debardieux and was the most successful of Les Indélicats.

Roger Falk was a painter, sculptor and an excellent draftsman. He was working in Le Musée de L'Homme as a graphic artist with Abbé Breuil, the French pre-historian and was a friend of professor Rivet, the creator and director of Le Musée de L'Homme. It is through my friendship with Falk that I was able to meet professor Rivet, who contacted me in Costa Rica and introduced me to Jacques Soustelle after the war. Falk spoke highly of my abilities to Rivet, who in turn later recommended me as teacher at the newly formed Franco-American Institute in Mexico City under Charles De Gaulle. I worked there briefly before coming to the United States from Costa Rica. Falk was arrested during the occupation, accused of helping Rivet escape from the Nazis in Paris. After several months, he was freed and returned to his job, but under surveillance. Falk was the instigator of Les Indélicats and led vital discussions and provided valuable advice. Lérouille and Falk were my closest friends.

Wagner was an engraver and went to Estienne, the best school of graphic art in France. He was a friend of Les Indélicats and a special friend of Adrien Cumura who went to Estienne with him.

Lantz was a decorator by trade and dedicated his life to cinema. He was an Alsatian, refined in his taste and manners, and the same bourgeois class as his friends, Lambert and Debarbieux.

Loiseau was a painter of porcelain. He was one of the earliest members of the group, more commercial than artistic, and somewhat obscure. He disappeared and then suddenly was with us again. He was the same age as Lerouille.

Gabriel Robin was the greatest painter of the group, but in my view without intelligence and morality. As a friend of Vlaminck, who encouraged him to paint, he was convinced that he was another *peintre maudit* (cursed painter). Robin was ungrateful and jealous of everybody, but he was a painter. When I began to make a better living in *orfèvre chez* Delsinne, Robin, when short of money, would come to ask me to buy one of his pictures. This explains why I had so many paintings of his first period. Visiting France after the war, I saw that he had changed his style, unhappily trying to be cubistic to please his galleries. He returned to repairing shoes in an effort to retain his independence. Robin wrote to me several times when I lived in New York, more disgusted and jealous than ever in connection with his exploitation by his galleries in New York and Canada.

Giselle Delsinne, was a daughter of Roger Delsinne. She came to work in her father's workshop as a chaser of gold and silver *orfèvre* persisting in a trade that is too hard for a woman. She was personally attracted to me and became one of Les Indélicats. Giselle married Adrien Cumura after the war and for me they were like family.

Adrien Cumura was one of the greatest engravers I have met in figure, relief and carving. He made exceptional portraits. Before the war he proposed marriage to Giselle and she refused. During the war, he was taken prisoner. Giselle proposed to him. As a married man he would have been permitted to leave the concentration camp and come back to Paris. Under the circumstances, he did not want to marry and thereby be grateful to the Germans, in spite of the fact that he had proposed marriage before the war. In my opinion, he was the inventor of monotype. He was painting in oil above a glass and afterwards transferring the painting onto paper that was specially prepared. Also, he was the printer of the *cahiers* with help from members and *vin ordinaire* at Rue Des Prairies. I was present just once during a printing. I respected Adrien as an artist and as a free man with high standards.

Magna, I didn't know well and I don't remember what he was doing or studying. I received a letter from him in Costa Rica asking me for information. I was attaché in the French Legation at the time. I didn't answer his letter because something about it was uncertain. Speaking with Falk about this letter after the war, Falk said that Magna was looking for contact. He was taken as a hostage, and afterward executed in the company of ten other innocents in retaliation for the killing of a German general. How terrible!

Marechal was attracted by the theater. He rarely met with Les Indelicats. He was the only member of the group with a communist tendency and that may explain why he was not often with us.

Ort was interested in decorative art. With his art school background, he was the man who after many discussions informed me of the cubist theory. It was about 1923. During the war all research had stopped. Before the war art deco was booming. Maybe the influence of my trade made it difficult for me to change. Thanks to Ort's reasoning, I started to make sculptures under cubist influence. After awhile, I felt that cubism was too limited, but I retained the lesson of construction. Recently, I saw an engraved silver-plated copper plate that I made in France in this period. I was also able to see two masks in aluminum, which I shaped by hammer and chased, where the African influence of the cubists is visible.

I took classes once a week for four years with a Professor Magne in the Conservatoire des Arts et Métiers. He was an architect. Referring to métier, he said that an artist has every right if one does something good and beautiful. Magne was in charge of conservation of historic monuments in France. Ort became an employee of *Vogue* Magazine.

Lambert, who studied at l'École des Arts Décoratifs, was an interior decorator and had his own business. He was intelligent and each time I saw him he was impeccably dressed and charming, a pleasant companion.

Oulbreck was an architect. He had a superior intelligence and a curious brain. Intrigued by architecture and attracted by scientific objects, he won first prize in a competition for an "affordable house." He disappeared in the war.

Gaude was a decorator of luxury yachts and also a product of l'École des Arts Décoratifs. He was the brother of the famous photographer who worked for Hovas News Agency. I spent a week's vacation with him at his brother's home in Marseille and was enchanted with both of them. Falk and I were invited to a soirée given by Gaude's parents in Paris. It was held in a salon of music. A singer, an aristocratic white Russian woman, performed to help ensure the life of her family. She had exceptional beauty and a superb voice. I still think of her today.

Les Indélicats expanded my thinking. They gave me other points of view beside those of industry. I was encouraged to explore and to think about aesthetics. I learned valuable new things in discussion with those fortunate to go to art school full time and to have leisure to work independently. But the discipline of my trade and of the workshop and my obligation to work shaped me. Les Indélicats were individualists and I liked their dedication to art, but I was not comfortable with their pranks and exhibitionism.

Chapter 8

Métier

Returning from military service, I was hired again by Opel, the chaser of bronze ornaments for furniture near Faubourg St. Antoine, with whom I soon fell into disagreement. Opel had asked me to find someone to replace me during my military service. The new chaser felt threatened by my presence and stirred up gossip and arguments. I left after one week.

Applying for work as a figurist, I assured a new employer that Volk had taught me very well. I looked so young he asked me if I had finished my apprenticeship. I was insulted and felt prostituted. He refused to accept my hourly rate saying that he didn't make that much himself. Then he asked me to come the following day; and he would see if I was worth my hourly rate. I was furious. In the morning he gave me *The Dying Slave* to chase, which I knew well, and sitting next to me, he took the same piece to make me feel his superiority. An hour and a half after the work began he realized that he was already far behind me. He abandoned the game and took another sculpture. At noontime he declared that I would receive the salary I had asked for. I said to him, "Thank you, but I am not staying here." Half of the day had passed and I asked him for my money. He wanted to know why I would not stay. I replied that I like to work where I can learn not teach. *Adieu!*

There is something I need to clarify regarding my métier. I have understood that from the Middle Ages, the quality of craftsmanship in France had been elevated and sustained uninterrupted for about one thousand years, longer than anywhere else. The guild-corporation maintained the highest standards of craftsmanship and a system of handing down knowledge and *tour-de-main* from master to companion. A companion made a tour of duty, *le tour de France.* (the tour of France, not to be confused with the modern bicycle race that started in 1903). He was called a *compagnon du duvoir*, meaning companion of duty symbolizing honor and work. He traveled around France and sometimes in other countries working at the side of a master in different workshops. He learned other techniques and styles and gained a wide comprehension of his trade. The tour continued for about for ten years.

When the companion felt ready, and if he was gifted, he earned the title of master by executing with his own hands a masterwork approved by the corporation. Only then was he able to open his own workshop, train apprentices and employ companions and masters. With the guild system, continuity of excellence was made possible. In brief, the corporations were powerful and became abusive. They were unable to see new trends with a good eye and were practically destroyed but not completely during the French Revolution.

In my time, guild traditions were practiced voluntarily in my métier and the situation was favorable to me at Volk's. Dieudome was a master who sat to my right and showed me all that he could. Moreover, I liked him. He was intelligent, cultured and amiable and he refrained from drinking. Volk sat to my left. A master recognized for his teaching trained Volk. This master was known in the trade as "George the Great." I remember meeting him. As I made my tour and worked in different workshops to increase my knowledge as well as to earn my living, I observed that the quality of the work being done was inferior. The owners were inferior artisans with enough money to open their workshops without knowing the trade and they accepted any kind of work, mining the conditions of work for the companions. Because of the misfortunes of war and being in the trenches, the companions did not have to apply their learning of the trade at the side of a master. When I left France, I felt the division between companions, masters and grand masters. Standards were lowered. The love and pride of the métier was lost.

There was another opportunity nearby. After arranging with the owner to start work the next day, George the Great, who was employed here, followed me down the street. He was upset. Now that I was hired, he was afraid to be laid off. I knew of his qualities, but at that moment he was old, alcoholic and sick. Under these circumstances, I was unable to take the job. He said, "Thank you Louis, I was sure of you." But the problem remained. I was just out of the service, married, and badly in need of money.

Finally, I returned to Lecouty. Business had picked up in his workshop. He now handled bronze ornamentation for furniture as well as statuary and employed about thirty-eight workers. His shop was modernized and efficient. He also had electricity. Lecouty had been friendly with me in the past and was delighted to find that I could do both figure and ornament. This was the beginning of a new period. At first the work was interesting, but quickly I recognized that it was too commercial. Here I was, caught in the middle of union mentality. I was a superior artisan, faster and better, but I was not paid more for the speed and quality of my work. Lecouty simply gave me more work to do and pressed for more speed from the others contrary to the norm in the workshop.

A solution presented itself. My bench was next to an elderly master by the name of Claret. He taught me how to make new tools in an entirely new way, which proved to be important to me. I observed that Claret was not in good health and suffered as a result of losing speed in production. Grateful for what this kind, knowledgeable man had already taught me, I found ways to help him maintain the necessary speed to legitimize his master's salary—and without the other men knowing it. I don't remember how long this lasted, but one day Claret said, "Louis, there is no future for you in a place like this with a *hand* like yours. Will you permit me on your behalf to visit the owner of the best workshop in Paris for chasing *orfèvrerie*?" I agreed. The next day he told me that the owner was waiting for me. Taking my courage by my two hands, I went to see Roger Delsinne, who would have a major influence in my future.

I brought with me two small bas-reliefs of landscapes with wild animals of America made in 1923. These were carved directly in bronze (*pris sur piece*). Delsinne was surprised and convinced that I was a chaser of quality. Considering my ignorance of *orfèvrerie* he did not want to promise to pay me the salary I was receiving at Lecouty, however he was glad to take me as an apprentice.

Most of the work done in this workshop was *repoussé* chasing of gold and silver. Once in a while an order came to the shop to chase a cast silver object. Delsinne recognized that I was able to do this specialty. No one in the shop had this capability. Delsinne was unable to do it well. He offered to pay my price for chasing a cast silver piece, but while I was learning *repoussé*, to receive the salary of an apprentice. He recommended that we work together.

Returning home, I questioned myself. Am I ready to start again? Am I willing to go through the deprivation of a low salary? In my conscience, I was convinced that it was an opportunity to increase my knowledge. Marguerite for once did not think about the money we would miss. By instinct, she pushed me to accept the plan. Coming to the workshop of Roger Delsinne in 1924 was the beginning of my life of work as a *sculptor-orfèvre*.

The workshop was in a brand new building at 19 Rue de Santoinge, a seventh floor walk-up with a pulley lift to hoist goods. Delsinne was the first occupant of this large studio, easily thirty by thirty-eight feet, with an adjoining office and a balcony where acid and plaster were handled. The windows were nine feet high. I had never seen a more beautiful studio. Lighting in the stairways was obtained from a gas jet burner that had the name *papillon* (butterfly) for when the gas was lit it formed a flame divided in two. It made one think of a butterfly.

Eventually, a larger area was lit by a gas jet with a hose, but it was fragile and often failed, to the despair of the boss. A gas lamp was placed in the middle of the workbench. In my métier, the workbench had the shape of an oak leaf, allowing five of us to work near one another. Our seats were placed in the hollows of the oak leaf to make the light brighter, the apprentices brought down from the shelf glass globes filled with water mixed with aniline. Each artisan had a globe in front of him and was thereby able to direct an even light onto his work reflected through the globe from the lamp in the middle of the bench. Only gold and silversmiths, jewelers and small businesses used this system. We heated with carbon coal. The first to arrive in the morning lit the pan, while the apprentices brought up the coal.

When electricity was installed the wires were run through the old gas tubes. The surprise came when electricity lit up the unclean corners of the room not seen before. The wall painting era had begun.

At times I seemed to be in the middle of hostility provoked by the esprit de corps of the gold and silversmiths; however I felt that Roger Delsinne was with me and that he had confidence in my ability. When orders came to chase silver casting, the other companions realized that they would be under obligation to accept me in their company. For a long time they called me *cuivreux*, an expression coming from copper instead of the respected and genuine name *bronzeur*. I was dedicated from the beginning of this experience and was determined to endure the insults without putting my master in trouble, understanding that he had to keep harmony between all of them. There were fourteen or fifteen chasers of *orfèvrerie*. It was definitely the best workshop of its kind in Paris.

Delsinne's brother Gaston, the only artist there, could have seen in me a serious competitor but he was far above the other companions and slowly he accepted the promise he saw in me to eventually become the best in the shop.

Another man, Julien Ometz, the most capable chaser I have ever known, was foreman of the Lechêne workshop before the war at Rue Du Cygne near Les Halles. During the last century and the beginning of this one, many excellent pieces of jewelry and were made here in the art nouveau style. When the war ended the wounded and the prisoners were sent home first. Roger Delsinne was seriously wounded and Gaston taken prisoner. Gaston was in the Lechéne workshop before the war broke out and this helps to explain why his brother Roger was able to buy the old Lechéne business. Ometz was hurt by this turn of fate. He never swallowed it. I believe that Ometz had a chance of being successor if he had not been at war when the shop became available. He died of cancer in 1925.

Before leaving for the hospital, Ometz told his wife, "If I don't come back, it is my desire that all of my tools go to Louis." This shows that his attitude toward me was different from the other gold and silversmiths in the workshop. He appreciated my desire to learn. Ometz was very important in my evolution as an artisan. With pleasure and honor I accepted these chests of tools. Since I was able to make my living, I paid the fair market value for them. I have always been proud to use them and to show them. Some of the chisels go back to the time of the French Revolution and have been handed down from master to master. Julien Ometz was an honest and good man.

The atmosphere in the workshop obliged me to swallow hostility from the other artisans but not always successfully. At times I was ready to physically fight, but attentive under the smile of Roger Delsinne, who would not have permitted a battle in his workshop. Since I was the only one ready to fight, everything stopped—no battle. The rest of the workshop was amused.

One day the order came to decorate vases with a frieze representing dancers, a copy of a Pompeian fresco. This moment was my chance. Beside Gaston, nobody was able to chase these figures. The first try by the companions was so terrible Roger asked them to stop. The anatomy and faces were a disaster. Roger then asked me if I was able to execute the work. I answered yes, without any doubt. We agreed that he pay me a value of eight hours of work per piece. I remember that three hours were enough for me per piece. The time left over was an opportunity to learn *repoussé* without losing salary. My progress was enormous as I had the advantage of having trained with a harder metal, bronze. My study of sculpture, drawing and anatomy came into play. All of this was from my past and when my dear Julien Ometz died, Roger was in need of my craftsmanship to replace him.

At Delsinne's in 1925, I chased a sword hilt of cast gold commissioned for Marshall Philippe Pétain and exhibited in the government exhibition called Expo Arts Deco. I heard that years later Pétain gave the sword to a church in Spain when he was the Ambassador to Spain. I chased another cast sword hilt in 1927. This one was in twenty-one karat gold with *The Smiling Angel of Rheims (L'Ange qui Sourit)*. It was for a director of the Musée du Louvre when he became a member of the French Academy. He was a specialist in medieval art and worked on Rheims Cathedral to repair war damage. Shortly after, I chased on a paten a profile portrait of the actor who portrayed Christ in the passion play at Oberammergau. Soon after, I chased a three-meter silver candelabrum for a customer in Holland.

It was 1926 when I returned home. My parents had moved to Belleville, where they had more space and a small garden. My father arranged my return secretly with my wife. I was angry at first but not for long. My mother was serving dinner. Looking at me with piercing eyes, standing still, holding a plate in her hand, she waited for me to come to her. This was in sharp contrast to the rest of the family pushing each other to embrace me. I was filled with emotion. Stupidly, I asked her if she was happy to see me again.

"Yes," she said, "But never would I have looked for you. When your father was at the window on the night you departed, I told him, 'Come to bed. Louis will not come back. I know him.'"

Then she said to me, "I have always had confidence in you, Louis. I knew that you loved your work and that you would have a life of achievement."

My father and mother retired to Rosny-Sur-Seine where he became mayor for eighteen years until his death in 1948. He was an incurable politician, and yet the same man who refused to be nominated socialist candidate because he would be obligated to vote with the party and perhaps contrary to his conscience. They built a two-story house with my sister Jeanne and her husband, Lucien. My sister Albertine, who never married, lived with my parents. Jeanne and Albertine worked as seamstresses well into their eighties. They worked for Paquin, a Paris designer of high fashion. Much against the family's will, Ernestine married a Spanish revolutionary. He died, and she married a Spanish florist. A Republican during the war, she became mixed up with Franco and was put into a concentration camp with her husband. My father guaranteed to take care of them. Losing all of their possessions, they were able to leave Spain, and go to Rosny. Ernestine worked in a bank and taught French in Spain and was a seamstress in France. Hard working like all the Férons, she had a great spirit.

In 1929, Delsinne received the famous order to chase a complete table service for King Fouad of Egypt for one hundred and twenty persons. All of the trade in Paris came to help us. This was a very good period for me. Roger agreed to pay me by the piece. I was able to deliver one to his taste in twelve hours instead of forty-eight and mine was better, with no need to retouch to give consistency and unity. I worked on the coffee-pot, teapot, chocolate pot and the largest serving pieces. This enormous order was received through Lapparra (Rue du Temple) and the same order was repeated for the Egyptian Embassy in Berlin. The model used was called Eudel, from the eighteenth-century French Regency. Needing money for war, Regent King Louis XV melted down his silver table service. Beforehand, a servant hid a coffeepot that was discovered about one hundred years later by a man named Eudel, who identified the original coffeepot from the original drawing. This coffeepot is in Le Musée Des Arts Decoratif. Delsinne's customers were either manufacturers (*fabricants*) or coordinators of *orfèvrerie*. I happened to learn the names of three of them beside Lapparra: Roussel, Broliquier and Cartier.

Things were going well. Every Sunday and holiday, I was free to use the studio for sculpture or anything I wanted to do. It occurred to me that if a silver coffeepot is made with a technique of raising metal by hammer over anvils (*monte au marteau*), then creating a three dimensional seamless sculpture is possible by going further with the principle used to shape the coffeepot. The cost of casting is thereby eliminated. Excessive weight is eliminated. The energy, unity and integrity of the artist's work are retained. It is now a question of skill rather than money. The concept ignited my imagination. No one in the Delsinne workshop knew how to shape metal by hammer over anvils. They were exclusively chasers. I wanted to sculpt a head of a woman in the round using half-red copper, a kind of bronze. The first try was unsatisfactory. Noticing a small crack on the back of the head I decided to cut away the defective part, mount it on a base, put it aside in the office and try again. One day coming back from errands, Roger informed that I had won first prize for figure in the 1929 Villemsen Competition. I was unhappy because I was not consulted and for me the piece was a failure; on the other hand the prize

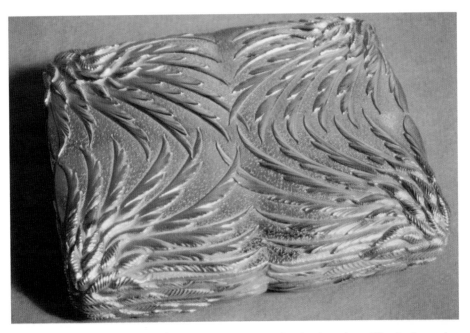

"Wing" Cigarette Box, 1970, 18 kt. gold, hammered with a feathered motif beginning at the corners and flaring out towards the center of the box, worked in repoussé. From a design by Jean Schlumberger. Unhinged. Marks: L.F.-H.S. (hors série; artist's model). Dimensions: 3 ¾ x 3 x ¾ in. Weight: 105.3 dwt. *Collection of C.R. Davis.*

"Meteor" Cigarette Box, 1970, 18 kt. gold, hammered and worked in repoussé and clicqueté. The rectangular box with a design of pointed forms is joined at the back by an invisible hinge. From a design by Jean Schlumberger. Marks: L.F. Artist's model for 24 meteor boxes made for a single client. Dimensions: 3 ¾ x 2 ⅞ x 1 ¼ in. Weight: 7 oz. *Collection of C.R. Davis.*

Above: *Sugar Bowl with Lid,* 1974, sterling silver, hammered, raised and worked in repoussé and ramoleyé, in the Berain or Eudel style; the bowl of squat hemispherical form, fluted at the corners, having a low domed lid and a hand wrought flower finial, all seated on a low flaring foot ornamented with heavy gadrooning. Marks: Louis Féron Feb 74. Height: 5 ½ in. Weight: 17 oz., 10 dwt.

At right: *Head of a Woman,* 1974, hammered and raised seamless from a single sheet of 22 kt. gold. Mounted on an ivory collar with gold ornaments. Verde antique marble base. Marks: Louis Féron 1974. Height: 10 ¼ in. *Purchased by Dr. Frank Reed. Permanent collection of Portland Museum of Art, Portland, Maine.*

COLOR PLATE 3

Sea Urchin Clock, 1966, gold clock case, 18 kt. gold, hammered and chased in repoussé for Schlumberger Dept. Tiffany, NY from a design by Nicolas Bongard. The case encloses a Bulova clock of 18 kt. gold with an accutron movement. Height: 2 ½ in. Weight: 54 dwt. *Collection of C.R. Davis.*

Plate, 1931, one of a kind piece. Copper gilt, hammered and chased, trace, ramoleyé, the plate of shaped circular form ornamented with designs taken from Berain, also called the Eudel, style. This piece won first prize for ornament cisele in the Thomas competition, Paris, 1931. Marks: Louis Féron. Diameter: 10 ¼ in.

The Dutchess, 1985. The body of 22 kt. gold worked in repoussé and chased ramoleyé resembles a chess piece. A diamond adorns the corsage. The head and neck are from one baroque pearl. Drop earrings are gold with one seed pearl. Cast base is also 22 kt. gold. Marks: L.F. Dimensions approx.: 3 x 1 ⁷⁄₈ in. Weight: 38 dwt. *Private Collection.*

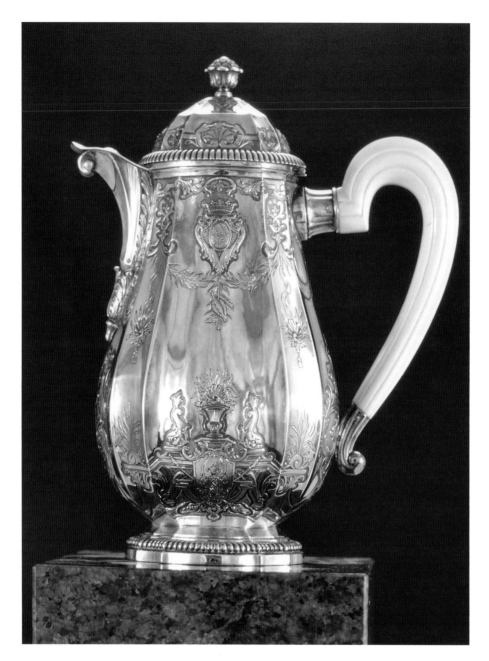

Coffee Pot, 1929, sterling silver, hammered, raised and worked in repoussé and ramoleyé, in the Berain or Eudel style. This piece won first prize from the City of Paris for ornament cisele in a period style in the Crozatier competition, Paris, 1930. The coffee pot of faceted baluster form, having a high domed lid above a gadrooned rim, terminating in a hand worked floral finial, having a hand carved ivory loop handle set into silver attachments, all on a shaped low base ornamented with a gadrooned rim. Marks: L.F. Height: 9 ½ in. Weight: 28 oz., 10 dwt. *Permanent collection of the Museum of Fine Arts, Boston, Art of Europe.*

"Wildflower" Necklace, 1970, 22 and 18 kt. gold. Hammered, worked in repoussé. American wildflowers ornamented with diamond bows set in platinum, also emeralds, sapphires and rubies. Marks: L.F. (and stamped). Dimensions: 7 ½ x 6 ½ in. *Collection of Mrs. Charles L. Stillman.*

The Four Seasons, 1969, coffret (glass box) of engraved glass panels held in a gold frame with flame and sunburst ornaments set with a large yellow sapphire. Chasse Orfèvrerier D'or for Steuben Glass. Gold 24, 22, 18 kt. Sapphire 56 cts. Height: 7 3/8 in.

At right top: *Ring,* 1970's. Sapphire and two precious stones set in gold. *Private collection.*

At right bottom: *Octagonal Box,* 1979, one of a kind piece. Sterling silver, hammered with 22 kt. gold. Hand wrought ornament on the lid depicting a spray of wild roses set with two diamonds, the lid bordered with a narrow gold band. Marks: L.F. Dimensions: 1 1/8 x 2 1/2 in. (diam.) Weight of silver: 60 dwt. (3 oz.) Weight of gold: 10 dwt. *Collection of C.R. Davis.*

Above: *Tumbler,* 1940, hammered silver chased ramoleyé. Height: 4 ³/₈ in. Weight: 98.2 dwt. Eudel in style. Made in Costa Rica.

Chinese Pavillion, 1974, glass, 18 kt. gold with precious stones and gold dragons on a base of agate. Designed by Donald Pollard, engraving design by Alexander Seidel, engraved by Roland Erlacher, goldwork by Louis Féron. Dimensions: 11 ¼ x 11 ¼ in. (diam.) *Commissioned by Steuben Glass. Two Chinese Pavillions were made. Both are in private collections.*

Unicorn, 22 kt. gold head, mane, tail, legs and body, with gold chain necklace. The marble base is accented by gold dots. Dimensions: overall - 2 ½ x 2 ½ in. (to tip of horn); ivory base: 2 ½ x 1 ¾ x 1 ½ in. high to tip of horn. *Private Collection.*

At right: *The Unicorn and The Maiden,* 1971, 18 kt. gold. Glass and gold design: Donald Pollard. Engraving design: Alexander Seidel. Engravings: Ladislav Havlik and Peter Schelling. Goldwork: Louis Féron. Dimensions: 14 ½ x 6 ¼ in. (diam.) *Made for Steuben Glass, Private Collection.*

COLOR PLATE 13

Above: *Teapot,* 1966, silver gilt, hammered, raised and worked in repoussé and ramoleyé in the Berain or Eudel style, with hand carved ivory handle. Marks: Louis Féron. Height: 8 ½ in. Weight: 26 oz., 9 dwt. *Private Collection.*

At right: *Two Female Statues with Bowls.* Two bronze figurines with gold details, lapis and pearls, set on natural rock with details of sea creatures in gold. *Private Collection.*

COLOR PLATE 15

Hands of Ivory, 1980s. Two hands hold a symbolic vase. Louis Féron. Height: 8 in. *Private Collection.*

COLOR PLATE 16

came with an amount of money that I was ready to accept and peace with Roger was restored.

Another sculpture that I made in the same technique pleased me, *Portrait of Joaquin Segura,* my Spanish brother-in-law, which I entered into the Crozatier Competition organized by the City of Paris in 1930. The jury declared that I won first prize and recommended that the Art Commission of the City buy this sculpture for a museum. I had an interview with the Commission chairman who expected a gift and said that I should be happy at my age to have a piece in a museum. I told him that it represented months of work and that I could not afford to give away so much labor. He commented. "You are very young. I have a legion of artists asking to have their work accepted free of charge." I signed a contract abandoning any right and was given a sum of money—about 2500 Francs—on top of the prize money.

I was starting to accumulate first prizes, so many in fact that after six or seven years these prizes gave me the right to enter the National Competition for Le Meilleur Ouvrier de France (M.O.F.), held every five years for trades with guild traditions and open to French speaking countries. I presented *Portrait of Jean*, a silver portrait hammered *monté au marteau*, seamless and chased in *repoussé* as the piece of my choice. The Committee of Reception required a piece of their choice, a bronze Bordeau cup, to be chased. Both works were accepted into the permanent collection of the Boston Museum of Fine Arts.

Always, Roger was behind me. There was a vacancy at L'École Boule for a professor of chasing. A competition was held to choose the next professor. It was a marvelous opportunity, twenty hours of work per week with good pay and time to sculpt. There was a requirement to stay *en loge* (in house) fifteen days. I accepted the sacrifice of two weeks without receiving salary. This competition was not only for chasing, but drawing, history of art, modeling and a demonstration of one's ability to communicate with pupils, which in this case was in front of all the members of the jury. I knew some of the members of the jury. They were surprised when I developed the theme of tools because I spoke about certain tools of which they were ignorant.

Shortly after, I went to L'École Boule where they were posting the results of the competition on a board and learned that I had the most points, but the director of the school, using his right, chose a pupil from the school who had never practiced the trade. He did not last as a professor at L'École Boule.

Coming back to the studio, everyone was looking at my face understanding that I was not chosen. I was rather discouraged. Roger, my guardian angel called me over to him and gave me a closed envelope addressed to him. I saw the post office date that was a long time before the date of the competition. Roger explained to me that he paid a visit to the director of L'École Orfèvrerie with an idea to recommend me. The director, who knew Roger well, asked him if this young artisan, meaning me, had a chance to win the competition. Roger said, yes. At this moment, Roger learned from the director that the name of the next professor was known.

Opening the letter, I read the name of the professor chosen; it was the same man who never practiced the trade. Naturally, I was in a rage. Roger told me that the director recommended he not say anything and to let me participate in the competition. Roger asked why. He answered, "This professor could be sick or have an accident in a taxi and besides they will know that this young man exists." As always, Roger was right.

Chapter 9

Resolution and Departure

I had the pleasure one day to meet Monsieur Contenot. He was the mayor of Paris. He was also an editor of Bronze d'Art and during the previous year he had been following my climb from my first competition. He gave a reception in the town hall of *arrondissement* III to honor me with the title of Meilleur Ouvrier de France. Frechet, the Director of L'École Boule, was invited to hand me the prize. Contenot introducing Frechet said, ". . . and Monsieur Frechet, who is always right, has simply missed Louis Féron as professor, today the best chaser of France." Contenot is the same man who during the Nazi occupation refused to shake hands with Laval, who was in the company of a German general in a reception at Hotel de Ville de Paris.

I remember that Contenot called to advise me not to leave France. He said that I was a link, a link between the old generation and the young who will come after. He tried to arrange to have the city of Paris buy pieces that I would be able to make in the future. I spoke of the Depression, and that I was working alone with Roger. Contenot offered me a post as professor in Hanoi, Indochina. I knew that he was a man absolutely from the Right, a conservative but not a fascist. I felt it best not to tell him why I refused his offer in Hanoi. I was thinking the Nazis would come with the excuse of destroying communism. I had observed the success of Franco in Spain and foresaw the war, perhaps not with Germany but certainly among Frenchmen. I was resolved to start my preparation for the trip to Costa Rica.

The Depression in France was making itself felt. An experience comes to mind. In Paris, on the corner of Rue Julien-La Croix and De Couronnes near the art school at Belleville, there was a dealer in second-hand goods—a junk shop. A young girl about fifteen years old was looking intently at a pair of silk stockings. This part of the street, in a poor area, is two steps from where Maurice Chevalier was born. The girl was emaciated and dressed in shabby clothing. She seemed too young to be thinking of becoming a prostitute. What she was lacking was food. Looking at her in ecstasy in front of a pair of silk stockings troubled me.

I thought of the difficulties I came out of. Here I was witnessing the feminine side of the same drama, the side that loses everything. I suffered at the idea of her future. It crossed my mind to buy the stockings for her but I was afraid to break her dream. And then I was unable to stay in front of the scene any longer and left feeling sad and disgusted without knowing why exactly. Arriving at the house, I spoke about it with Marguerite. She said, "You are foolish, Louis. I am certain that she would have been unhappy if you had proposed buying them for her." But why remains a mystery. I regret not expressing how I felt—to the young girl and to my wife.

Roger and I were the only craftsmen left in the workshop. In a certain measure we were in competition with one another. He was trying to keep his advantage, his age and position, and was unwilling to share with me. In spite of the problem, I was enjoying more time to work on my sculpture, to visit art exhibitions, to go to the theater and to study at La Grande Chaumière and Collarosi Academies. The Delsinne workshop was practically my own. *Les Indélicats* were welcome, sometimes showing movies or meeting for reunions.

We were living in fast moving times. The schools of art were changing almost before they were fully created and this half misery seemed to be favorable for artists. Many arrived in Paris from the East, from Germany and Russia, Jewish and non-Jewish. Some were already famous and others were fleeing from the Nazis. I met a lot of these artists and they were stimulating people. It was an exchange of ideas that I never expected.

Speaking of dynamic influences, Wagner moved me deeply. Playing his compositions was forbidden until after the war. Finally, on Boulevard de Sebastepol, a concert was held once a week directed by a violin-cellist giving parts of Wagner's repertoire. This made me so happy that I left all the other composers for a rather long time. Today I take great pleasure from his works without neglecting other great ones, whose music was impossible to hear during my years in Paris.

An earlier experience was at the Labor Exchange near Place du République where Albert Doyen conducted the *Pastoral Symphony* of Beethoven with chorus and without any musical instruments. I was alone with my father. For us and especially for me in my innocence, it was an awakening—what an evening!

Peer Gynt was performed at the Theater of the Renaissance on Grande Boulevard conducted by Pierre Monteau, whom I met years later in New York. During our discussion I told him that I was present at this performance in Paris. "Impossible," he said, "You weren't born." He was surprised at my age. I expressed what I saw and felt and have remembered. He commented that Grieg's *Peer Gynt*; the music and the theme, had always impressed him.

When I entered the amphitheater of the Sorbonne with my mother, father and Marguerite in 1933, I knew that I was going to receive the highest degree that an *orfèvre* was able to dream about, if his gifts permitted this in his lifetime. I was thirty-two. I was proud, yes, but during the past years leading to this day I had neglected my parents and Marguerite. For me it was an excuse to show them that it was not from egotism that I had acted this way. I still see the faces of my mother and father fixated on me at the call of Louis Féron to be named Commander of the Ordre du Travail. I left my seat and walked up onto the stage. After words of introduction, President Lebrun of France was handed the tie and placed it around my neck. I saw the crowd as through a fog. I went down to rejoin my parents. They were not able to speak, nor was I—their eyes were full of tears. All the pains, all the efforts, all the little treasons were erased. It was a grand emotion. I hope that I have been forgiven.

After the ceremony at the Sorbonne, an exposition was held. My principal work was next to that of a carpenter. He was surprised by my piece, and asked me many questions and about my tour. I was speechless in front of his masterwork. He had made a church in wood. It measured two meters in height and showed to scale all of his capacities, deliberately combining three styles. I remember how happy he was. He had won the title of best carpenter of France. There were many trades represented. This enormous hall was filled with men who I am certain were as uplifted as the two of us. Each one wore a sash with the three colors of France and decorations attached to his jacket. It was a spectacle of color that made me imagine the tournaments of the Middle Ages.

Shortly after I won the title of Meilleur Ouvrier de France, I was introduced to Gimond, a sculptor of quality and professor at Les Beaux-Arts. Gimond was friendly with me. Looking at pictures of my work, he advised me to present one of my pieces, a life-sized hammered bust of a man in half-red copper in the juried exhibition of Les Indépendants at Le Petit Palais. Thinking of the jury I was doubtful, keeping in mind that I was not coming from the official school, Les Beaux-Arts. In any event, Gimond, being part of the jury, promised to help me. I received the necessary papers to be accepted in the exhibition.

On Varnishing Day, I discovered that my sculpture was next to a piece by François Pompon. In my opinion, Pompon is the greatest sculptor of animals since the Egyptians. It was a parakeet. The name of the bird is Ara, which he carved from a block of onyx-verte from Brazil. It is such a beautiful form and so rich. I was flabbergasted in front of his work, without noticing that he was observing me. He asked me, "Where is your work?" He looked at it and congratulated me, admiring the technique involved. Pompon was a great practitioner. He passed all his life making a living executing marble works for sculptors who were too busy or incapable to carve their own work. After a moment he invited me to go with him to see the entire show. In stature he was a little bit smaller than I was and already seventy-eight years of age. He took my arm and I felt that he would not have made this big tour without assistance. Going along commenting, we were exchanging histories of our lives. I felt so free with him that I indiscreetly asked him what he was asking for Ara. He told me the price that represented two or three years of my salary. He looked at me and said, "I don't need money anymore. I have always been poor, and for a long time was not able to get married. Now, I have habituated my stomach to eat very little, two eggs and a glass of milk."

As I was speaking with him about the universal admiration of his work, he said that he would leave his pieces to the city of Paris, but forbid reproduction into commercial editions. I was invited to his *atelier* and visited him two or three times. I can still see the plaster models on the shelves, plenty of them, and some sculptures on the stands. During his lifetime, his work was admired. He was a carver employed by Rodin. Late in his career, an architect visiting his *atelier* admired the study of his famous white bear, *L'Ours Blanc*, and told him the sculpture would be marvelous if he could enlarge it. Pompon answered that he had no money to buy the stone. The architect promised him that he would receive the necessary block as a gift. The rest was in his hands. After Pompon made *L'Ours Blanc*, all the world knew him. He died in 1933, not long after the exhibition and one year before my departure to Costa Rica. Beside my admiration for his work, I keep a memory of this artisan who served Art like a saint of a religion.

The first exhibition I saw of Antoine Bourdelle was at Rue de La Boétie. To my way of thinking, he is the best sculptor of his period, more of a sculptor and less of a modeler than his friend Rodin. He had a sense of architecture that is rare. His works gave me such a strong impression that I felt cold in my stomach. Rarely have I experienced such a feeling. I do not know how to define this thing. It is like a wound. Since then, I have seen his works numerous times in Paris and with Leslie when I had the freedom to spend the time I believe necessary to observe them.

Another great artistic emotion that affected me to the point of shock was *Le Pas-d'Acier* performed at the Theater Châtelet. My seat was behind a column and so as not to lose anything of this marvelous spectacle a movie was provided. The dancers who were in the front occupied the whole scene, advancing from one side then from another. I felt that they were going to come down into the orchestra and upon us. Everyone in the audience stood up as one being. This was a communion.

I made sacrifices in order to see the maximum number of Russian ballets. These accumulated experiences laid a foundation of art that I knew I would need for my future—a future that I never doubted.

Marguerite left France with my tools in order to prepare a place for us in Costa Rica. In the worst weather imaginable, my departure was fifteen days later, going first to London and then to New York on the ship *America*. The captain and I and one other passenger were the only ones in the dining room. I arrived in New York four days late and stayed with the son of a friend, a young medical student at Columbia University, for two weeks waiting for a boat from the United Fruit Company, *Le Peten*, which would take me to Port Limon, Costa Rica. I had made these two stops to see if there were opportunities in London or New York in my métier. The Depression was worse than in France and the bread lines were long in New York. The companions who I met did not encourage me. When I arrived in San José I knew that "my boats were burned." I must be ready to prove my worth to myself and decided not to minimize my efforts in any way.

Chapter 10

Costa Rica

The trip from New York to Limon had been like a dream, speaking neither English nor Spanish and being rather like an adopted person. Several passengers were friendly with me, including some young women who spoke French. The daughter of the Governor of Jamaica invited me to visit her father. Another, who became a friend, was the daughter of an architect in Detroit. Mr. K. invited me to follow him to Detroit where the sculptor Mills worked and said he would see what he could do for me, etc. I had just arrived. I was still on the boat and the second day there was an offer to leave without knowing what I could do in Costa Rica. It seemed as if he was interested to buy me for his daughter, who did not disguise her attraction for me.

The first days in San José were spent looking for a suitable place for my studio. My tools were waiting for me and I was optimistic. There was a succession of visits from people familiar with French and with France. The first one, I believe was a General Volio, a former Catholic priest living alone in Saint Anna in a superb house full of books.

It was a big pleasure to be in his company, exchanging ideas and remembrances. He had been formed in a seminary in San José and at Louvain, Belgium, under the guidance of Cardinal Mercier, who during the First War was recognized as a hero defending innocent people. General Volio was the brother of Bishop Volio, who was also the brother of the President of the Chamber of Deputy—three Volios in charge of the state. Their characters provoked a fear of seeing a formation of a dynasty. The two religious men, the ex-priest and Bishop Volio, suffered from this fear.

The general was without a doubt a superior person. I have often thought of his ancestors who I understood came from Italy. He was a man of the Renaissance, a *condutere* affective in obscurity. His brother, the bishop, became a good friend and protector, promptly dedicating his efforts to help me. He had been sent to Honduras as a bishop but became involved in a revolution in Nicaragua. He was injured and returned sick to Costa Rica. Because he abandoned his position he was named *in partibus*—without party. The general, learning that his brother was in the revolution in Nicaragua, abandoned his habit as priest and went there to offer his military service.

Without losing time, the guerrilla gave him a job to participate in an attack. He had been educated in Europe and when the order came to attack, he went ahead but no one followed. Suddenly he found himself in the middle of two camps; the nearest being the enemy. The guerrilla was not risking. It was like this. So he continued alone and was able to conquer the position. Immediately the people followed him. They decided he must be a general. He lived the rest of his life as General Volio. He was a priest with character; very intelligent but dramatic like a cultured Italian *gondaturie*. When I left Costa Rica he was in charge of the archives of the nation. He could do anything well but was a kind of rebel. Because he abandoned his place as a priest, he was excommunicated by Rome, but later pardoned and, being Catholic, authorized to receive communion. No doubt he was suffering not to be able to go to church. He was a superior man and became a very special friend. Now his brother, the Bishop, introduced me to President Ricardo Jiménez Orea Meno.

The idea of meeting with President Jiménez was to thank him for permitting me to bring all of my tools to Costa Rica without paying duty. It was an excuse to meet him. He received us graciously and Bishop Volio translated our interview. The President was asked if he could do something to enable me to stay in Costa Rica. I keep in my memory one of the most remarkable men I have met in my life. He asked me very politely if I desired to teach what I know. My answer was yes. He said, "Monsignor Volio, why don't you take Monsieur Féron to the Ministry of Public Works and speak with the secretary, Don León Cortés Castro?" Don León Cortés was a candidate for presidency and happy to be of service to a big personality like the bishop and to attach himself to a good element and perhaps find a position in the School of Public Works.

It was necessary to learn Spanish in order to give my classes. The secretary of the French legation, Pierre Ducuron, offered to teach me. He came to Costa Rica as a child and learned to speak Spanish perfectly. Costa Ricans wondered if he really was a Frenchman because he spoke as they did. Every evening after his dinner he instructed me and was faithful as a professor and as a friend. Four months of study followed. Realizing that I was beginning to speak sufficiently well he said, "Louis, tell me, how do you intend to teach your classes?" He perfected what I proposed and five months after my arrival in Costa Rica I was with my young pupils. The salary was reasonable, with the right to have my own workshop. I was busy from the seventh hour in the morning until eleven for the government. The rest of the time I was free to work on commissions.

Meanwhile, Bishop Volio introduced me to the priest in charge of the Basilica de Nôtre Dame Des Angeles that was preparing to make the Tri-Centenaries of the Apparition of the Virgin. After several miraculous experiences at this location a basilica had been built. Monsignor Volio and the priest asked me to make a chalice, to be paid for by a national subscription, and gave me information about the festival. The design was left to me but with the understanding that the five republics of Central America be included. I returned from Cartago with Monsignor Volio ignited with an idea, having listened well to all liturgical recommendations. Arriving home I was ready to prepare my drawing for the chalice and the paten, which were subsequently presented and accepted.

Old silver objects of cult were given to me to be melted and refined by the son of an *orfèvre* in Cartago, who delivered the metal clean and ready to be worked, but it was rough and not of good quality. Before leaving France, I bought silver just in case and this was used for the chalice that I believe today to be a big piece of my work. The Last Supper was depicted, the symbol of each of the five republics and the monogram of Christ in the front. The paten represented the Apparition of the Virgin.

Before the chalice was consecrated, President Jiménez received me in the middle of a cabinet meeting. He requested that one of his ministers give me his chair. Everyone seemed surprised by the beauty and quality of my work. The President was charming, as I have always known him to be.

I returned home exhausted, having worked hard for a long time without rest knowing the deadline was near. I stretched out on my bed and went to sleep. Suddenly awakened by a loud knock; I opened the door. In front of me was an officer dressed like a French general. I was completely stupefied, forgetting the little bit of Spanish I was able to communicate. Then I realized the car outside had the symbol of the arms of the country and was the car of the President who was coming with his wife and sister in law to see the chalice. I was able to find my spirit more or less and to receive them the best I could, explaining something about the work to Señora Jiménez, who was most respectful and happy to be permitted to touch the chalice before its consecration. The President inquired about my wife. I said that she was in town buying something for the window and that I was sorry not to know about his visit; otherwise she would have been here. "No, no; it's not important. I will come back. I want to meet her."

After a while, Marguerite returned and I told her about the visit. She was dejected and decided that we should return the visit. Thanks to the French legation I was able to get an appointment. The president, *un grand seigneur*, stood up and came to the door to offer his hand to Marguerite and in correct French to welcome her to Costa Rica. He was showing so much good will that I took the liberty to say that I was surprised that he let me fight for my Spanish. He answered with a smile; "Men are made to fight. With women, it is different." So, naturally I kept quiet. Each time we happened to meet one another in the street of San José, he never failed to change his route, to remove his hat and to salute Marguerite. The last memory I have of this gentleman is on the day that I was saying goodbye. Leaving the people I owe the pleasure and the honor to have been able to work with in Costa Rica and to be appreciated—eleven years of joy. I cannot forget it.

Don León Cortés, ex-secretary of Public Works, was the man who gave me the job to teach drawing, geometry and applied arts. He became president of the republic in 1936. After a short time, he visited the workshop of the Public Works and my class, asking me if I was content. I told him frankly that I was grateful to have a job and that if something could be changed, I would be pleased to do more for the pupils. He was a lawyer by trade and listened quietly. After a pause he asked, "Would you be interested to create and take care of a school of apprentices of Public Works?" Happy with my affirmation he said, "So, Féron, prepare your project. Come to see me as soon as you can and we will decide."

Meanwhile, I asked the French legation to provide me with all the information possible regarding the classes where I studied at night in France. Quickly I received the information and changed what needed to be changed to comply with the town and country. After thinking it through, I asked for an interview with the director of the Public Works. The new president, Don León, was very attentive and sympathetic. The project was pleasant for him and speaking together he promised to have a school and a chapel built near the workshop of Public Works. I designed the chapel and the pupils decorated it with their teacher. It is well-cared for and full of flowers. This chapel touched Leslie when we made our visit in 1987.

There is something remarkable to me that occurred during the discussion with the president to establish the rules of the school. Already knowing the milieu relatively well, and the young people who would come to the school, I proposed giving them a salary for the first three years plus something more for the fourth year. This would relieve problems for their families and keep them in school. He accepted the idea and was absolutely ecstatic, because in his opinion the school was for the underprivileged so that they could advance socially and be useful in the nation. He never missed a chance to come to speak with them and to tell them his dream for their country. The president and I developed a mutual sympathy. The success of the school was making him very happy.

I was paid as a secretary of state, exactly half because I worked only in the morning. When the President asked me to make a sculpture for the school, the customhouse, the house of lepers, ambassadorial gifts or a portrait, I was always paid separately for each project. He gave me the impression that he was enchanted with my work. One day he sent his limousine to the school. Everyone was asking why his limousine was sent. The students at the school were beginning to make forged ironworks for the Sabana airport. At the time I was working with them on a metal door. A master mechanic, Umberta Regas, as a friend of Don León, had interested the President in the Sabana airport project; consequently I went to the Presidential Palace directly in his limousine. He asked me if I had an idea of how to decorate the reception room of the airport. As it was my job to go there often I had been dreaming about the reception room. Almost without hesitation I proposed to sculpt a stucco bas-relief depicting the history of Costa Rica. This is marvelous because like all of the Costa Ricans I met, he never asked me if I was able to do it. He said, "Go, Don Louis, bring me your project so that we can work together."

After measuring the walls and windows of the airport salon, I stopped my classes, entrusted them to the master of the workshop and withdrew to my studio. Without delay I presented my drawing to the president. He was enchanted with what I showed him and made some remarks about Costa Rican history. After that he said, go ahead, don't lose time. The president gave me the order and the permit to take a mason, Francisco Jiménez, who had good taste and had decorated the chapel of the school. I had several reasons to appreciate him. Everything became like my dream. All the necessary materials were coming, the help, the money from the government and my salary was not touched. This was truly a big adventure for me.

Francisco was very capable. We had worked together several times on artistic projects: the four pendentives and baptismal font in the church of St. Terisita, the school in St. Ramon, and the customhouse at Puntarenas. This man was happy to work with me. He was not jealous. He never demonstrated that he considered me a foreigner and he was in love with the work. In short, we were working well together. We decided upon the size of the stucco panel that he would prepare in

La Sabana Murals, 1940, carved stucco bas-relief murals gilt, covering 1500 feet of the Diplomatic Salon at the International Airport, San José. Commissioned by President of Costa Rica, Don León Cortés, in 1940. In recent years the airport terminal was closed and transformed into Museo de Arte Costarricense, housing the murals where Féron received a citation from the government of Costa Rica in 1987.

advance for me, then waited for a certain moment when the stucco was tough enough to trace my figure, and firm enough to carve. I started to carve the bas-relief. It was like a fever.

A pupil of my evening drawing class, Raphael Rodriquez, sensitive to art, was studying in the university to become a professor of natural history. He was invaluable when I had to choose an animal or plant according to the date, particularly the pre-Columbian period, or during the time of the Conquest. Well educated in the States when he was young, Lucas was enormously helpful when I prepared my papers for application for a visa to the United States in 1945. I was happy to make his portrait in bronze before leaving Costa Rica. I believe it is now in the Museo De Arte Costarricense in Savana, San José.

Every day at six-thirty in the morning I was on the scaffolding carving the wall. I was young, thirty-nine years. When feeling fatigued, there was Costa Rican coffee and a good French cognac. I worked until eleven at night—to bed and a fresh start in the morning. During the day, there were visits from society. They didn't go to the circus; they came to see me. I would make an excuse of being full of plaster. My helper explained that it was worse for me to go down from the scaffolding. I would go down according to a sign from him. When the former President Ricardo Jimenez arrived, I went down. One day the President León Cortés came to visit. He looked around and offered his felicitations. He asked me when the work would be finished. I answered that I did not know. He told me that his presidency would end at such a date and that the new government may not be disposed to pay for the work that is mine. I understood and worked doubly hard finishing on time and was promptly paid. Everyone was happy except a politician from Cartago who could not stop finding defects. His friend answered, "Maybe it is not running fast, but it is a big horse." He was really the only one who was not happy with my work, this imbecile.

Doctor Calderon Rafael Angel Guardio succeeded León Cortés as President of Costa Rica in 1940. He was a medical doctor educated in Belgium, married to a Belgian woman and pro-French. He was also pro-American without problems with the United Nations because the pro-American influence was stronger than in the term of León Cortés, who was surrounded with Germans. Between us I learned of the visit of Monsieur

Bardier, the ambassador of France in Central America. In the presence of Fisseux, who was chargé d'affaires in Costa Rica, I received from Bardier the offer to be named, Cultural Attaché of the French Legation. As I was thirty-eight at the time and in good physical condition, being called to the army in Martinique was a possibility. It never happened. I don't know exactly to whom I owe this good luck. León Cortés received the ambassador, Calderon, and Fisseux and certainly he learned what I had done in favor of French propaganda. Perhaps the cost of transport and a pension to my wife during an absence in Martinique was considered to be too expensive. This is my opinion. I was honestly happy to escape all of the trouble of abandoning what had been established in Costa Rica.

One day at the legation, Bardier telephoned me because he leaned that Pétain, the new man taking care of the government in Vichy, asked from all of us the oath of fidelity—and also the addresses of Jewish residents in Costa Rica. This was in 1940. The three of us in one voice refused. Under these circumstances, Fisseux tried to make contact with Soustelle in Mexico (Jacques Soustelle was a personal delegate of General De Gaulle.) I knew Soustelle from Le Musée de L'Homme where Falk was working. On the phone, Soustelle asked me to stay in contact with Pétain and to inform him, Soustelle, of what Pétain might ask. I refused. I am not the type. Soustelle said in this case, he would make a visit to see me and ask me to found the Free French in Costa Rica, and to put me in contact with the English legation. This occurred. Andrea Challe became president and on August 2, 1941, I became secretary.

Sometime later, Fisseux asked me to come to the legation to show the dossier of each one. Mine, I remember, said, "First Orfèvre of France." I was not openly declared an anarchist, but I was belonging to a certain *d'avant guarde*—without doubt repeated from the consierge in Paris where I was the only one who was not a *Croix de feu*. Louis Féron was not an anarchist and not a *crois de feu*. He belonged to a certain *d'avant guarde*. Féron's dossier reinforced Féron's opinion of the French during the occupation. "If you were neither communist nor fascist you were accused of being an anarchist."

I received from Garand Dambale, ambassador of the Free French in Mexico, a letter and a diplomatic passport, having lost my papers as a result of not signing an oath of fidelity to Pétain in Vichy. I believe the letter arrived in San José in 1944, and I remember that it was not an invitation. It was presented like an order. I was to be a professor of *orfèvrerie* at the Instituto Franco-Americano in Mexico. Dr. Rivet was the director at this time. He knew me in Paris when he was the director of Le Musée de L'homme. After finishing the works I was in charge of in San José, I decided to take a chance in this position, although seriously doubtful of the outcome.

Tabernacle, 1942, sterling silver hammered and chased tabernacle, Romanesque in style. Dimensions: 40 x 48 in. Weight over 107 pounds. The entire piece is made by hand with no casting and is the largest silver work by Féron. It includes 12 apostles, 3 saints, 4 evangelist symbols, 2 angels, crosses and grape leaves and fruit ornaments all of which are chased au repoussé. It is an interpretation of St. Trophime at Arles, France. Commissioned for La Agonia Church, Alajuela, through popular subscription. Signed Louis Féron. Made in Costa Rica.

Chapter 11

Gaullists in Mexico and the Personalities of San José

En route to Mexico from San José, I took a plane to Guatemala where Ducuron was consul under Medioni, an Ambassador of the Free French. I spent one night there. The abode was rather beautiful with an excellent wine cellar. It was formerly occupied by the German legation before the rupture with Germany. Medioni and I remained good friends. We met in Paris several times when I was there on business and he told me that he would renounce his present post as ambassador of Madagascar because the General was "too much." He returned to the University of Nice and became a doctor of acupuncture, I believe with success.

We arrived in Mexico in torrential rain, having passed through a violent storm. It appeared that lightning hit the wing of the plane. I took my bags and went to the hotel American where I later telephoned a filmmaker for *The March of Time*, Marcel Rebiere, who had written to me. He was in the middle of preparing leek soup and invited me to come over. The taxi driver understanding that I had just arrived took me for a good ride. The next day it became evident to me that Rebiere's hotel was one hundred meters from mine.

Visiting Garand Dambale and Dr. Rivet, who both treated me kindly, it was explained that I would be under the orders of Preforcat, a *sculptor-orfèvre*, the son of the famous *orfèvre* of Paris. Preforcat had the same admiration that I have for our field of work. In a short time we became friendly. He was saying to me that in Mexico he had the most intelligent workers he had met in his life. I told him how much I appreciated the fact that his father was the only one to fight against plots to find a reason to prevent me from competing in France, and to wait five years for the next National Concours. I was young and winning the title was the crown of a career. He agreed with Delsinne, who thought it was good because I deserved first place. While the young Preforcat did not know about this, he had seen the quality of my work in photographs given to Rivet and said, "Louis, I told Rivet that when Féron arrives in Mexico, I will renounce directorship. I will be happy to be with him but not to be his boss."

Then I began what I was employed to do. Nothing advanced. There were endless discussions. These French intellectuals, however, were undoubtedly highly thought of and waiting for the situation to arrange itself in France in order to regain their advantage, their "butter plate." Like me, they received a salary. I would say a generous one that was helpful in a foreign country cut off from their means in France. I also understood that France was interested in saving her patriots.

A letter from Costa Rica informed me that Marguerite needed an operation on a small tumor. I asked the ambassador if he would grant me a leave of absence to return to San José. At this time, Algeria was liberated. Not all of the French politicians in Mexico were able to keep their places. Rivet left first. He was a deputy before the war. De Gaulle hastened to reunite those elected in France to fight against the efforts of the English and Americans who wanted to place people whom they favored. We had a reunion to choose the new director of the university. The best person was Jules Romin, a publicized writer. Everyone asked him to take the head job. He responded, "Not I, I have a name. If something happened to me at the university, my name would be affected.

Everyone would listen to that. The only one is Féron." It is certainly the memory of this reunion for the succession of Rivet that made me regret to leave Mexico. I must say that during these four months, I appreciated the artistic and intellectual milieu that I found here.

A reception was held at the Romanian consulate and Rebiere was there taking pictures. He had been present in Romania before the war and during his filming became friendly with King Carol. Rebiere insisted upon introducing me to his majesty, who had heard about me and wished to meet me. Truly, not to vex anyone, I consented to be introduced.

Surrounding King Carol was a real court waiting to return to Romania. I say with pleasure that this man appeared to me to be democratic. And also, speaking French with me he demonstrated an interest in my life as an artist. Surveying the court he said, "I would like to introduce you to my wife." Thus he drove me _____ to introduce me. She was petite, especially next to King Carol, and she was dressed in white. I have never seen such a neck and bust in my life. I was fascinated with her. She was saying to me how much she loved France and the French. With regret I asked to take her leave. She wished me success and health. What a woman—what a memory I have of her.

Perhaps I left an opportunity in Mexico, but at the same time I understood that the altitude would not permit me to do the great physical work that I loved to do. And, I was not made for a career as a functionary. Dambale accepted my resignation. I returned to San José and started to work again.

A remarkable man who honored me with his friendship was Monsigneur Victor Sanabria Martinez of Alajuela. I met him early. When he became Archbishop and Prelate of Costa Rica I was asked to make six pieces for him; a crosier, a pectoral cross, a mission cross, two ecclesiastical rings and the archbishop's seal. This gave me an opportunity to become well acquainted. I held him in high esteem, as the head of the church and as a friend. The Episcopal palace was on the way to my studio and as neighbors our paths often crossed. Leaving the *curé*, I would see him return to the house. Sometimes he stopped and asked me to accompany him to the palace where he offered me a small glass of wine.

It was a mental rest for me to be in his company. One day I asked if he could help me to receive full payment for the silver tabernacle I made in Alajuela, my largest silver work. It was a commission through popular subscription. He said that I must go to the court and that I would win. I learned later on that his entire fortune had been distributed to the poor and that raised my opinion of him even more.

I have a truly good memory of Charles Lancaster, who gave to science the greatest number of orchids. We met during a flower exhibition where both of us had been chosen as judges. He was English. We got along so well, a faithful friendship developed. He disappeared, busy somewhere in South America, but came back to live in Cartago, which he chose for the climate. It was favorable for growing orchids. He never missed a chance to pay me a visit. One day he learned through the newspaper that I was leaving for Mexico. He said that he regretted my departure and wished to give me something in memory of our friendship. He asked me if I had ever read Edgar Allan Poe's "The Golden Scarab." I said yes and that Poe was an author who I liked. A discussion began. He said the world was convinced that the scarab was Poe's invention. One day looking for orchids in Panama he stumbled on a scarab exactly as described by Poe. It was a discovery. "Louis. I am going to give it to you." I didn't know what to say or what to do. I did accept this present. After six months or so I returned from Mexico and Charles paid me a visit. We were happy to see each other again and I said that perhaps I should return the golden scarab. He said no because he would not give it away again. When I left for New York I learned of his death in Costa Rica.

I remember well a visitor to our house in San José. His was a Spanish gypsy, nervous like the string of a musical instrument. He had escaped from Spain with the statue of the black Virgin of Malaga after the communists had violated the cathedral, stealing the jewels that adorned the relic. He asked me to redo the crown and scepter. He had traveled through Latin America collecting silver and some stones and thought he had enough to fulfill his promise to the *Negrita*. I accepted the project with joy. When I asked that he bring me the object to know the proportions and the size of the head he broke into a rage of hysteria. To reassure him, I told him that an *orfèvre* has the authority from the

Catholic Church to touch all sacred objects. He protested vigorously. This went on for one hour. Never have I experienced anything like it. Then finally he ended up believing me and promised to bring me the Virgin Saint. He arrived the next day like a plotter, all dressed in black. He also brought his silver and precious stones for me to use to reconstruct and to decorate the *Negrita*.

Shortly after, he presented me with two tickets to his recital at the National Theater. I admired his gifts as an actor and musician. He accompanied himself with a guitar reciting verses from Spanish poets. Everything was going well until the moment he said something in favor of Franco. The audience was divided into two, the Republicans and the followers of Franco. I had friends in both and was confirmed in my opinion that nobody can change them. To this day, I like the Spanish people I have met. I love their courage, their frankness and their nobility. With them one does not need to look behind to see if they are with you when they have made a promise to go with you in any adventure. The day I was completing the work, he embraced me and said that he was leaving and asked that I deliver the piece to his hotel.

I walked up to his room that was not clean and in disorder. He was still in bed. I offered to leave but no, no, he was getting up. What a spectacle—without shaving or at least washing his face and still in bed he began to accumulate his medals of saints. I don't know how many but this went on for a half an hour kissing each one and making the sign of the cross on his eyes, mouth and chest between his skin and his dirty shirt. Witnessing this fanatic demonstration I thought of Sanabria's remark, "Louis, let each one drink from the river according to his means—from a vase or a shell or from his hands." The *Negrita* was returned to Malaga embellished with my work. The victory of Franco had opened the doors for him.

I have been proud and happy to live among people who value freedom, a freedom that each person has a right to have. In Costa Rica, I lived a life of work that I had dreamed of as a young man, using all of my capacities for people who appreciated them. I had the pleasure of producing work for four presidents: Don Ricardo Jiménez, Don León Cortés, Dr. Calderon Guardio and Theodore Picarde, all of whom were like protectors to me. I believe the circumstances of the war in France and my departure from politics helped me. The change of presidency never interfered with the flow of work. By nature I detest things that are not clear. All of the works for the government or for the people who have honored me with their orders were commissioned without deals and promises and without losing my dignity. I am thankful to each of these presidents and to all of the Ticos who made me feel that I was one of them.

The friends I made in Costa Rica remained friends. One day, in my studio a young man, Henri Agnel, presented himself. Undoubtedly he had been informed that I was French and wanted the assurance that I was French. We engaged in conversation. He was from Marseille and was a pilot in South America after being the personal pilot of Chiang Kai-shek. I remember seeing a passport in silk that he kept. This was around 1937 or 1938. He had gone back to France at the beginning of the war and was in a company near the Pyrenees. Without asking authorities for opinions or permission he personally flew planes to Algeria one by one until there weren't any more. This is right above Spain.

He went to England and offered his services and was put in charge of the Ferry Command until he realized that he was receiving an inferior payment because he was French. On his refusal to continue, the English asked him to assure the connection of planes between Miami and English possessions. During the war, I saw him often in San José where he stopped to refuel his aircraft. After the liberation of Algeria, he continued his métier there and married a pied-noir. We saw one another in New York when he was flying from Paris to New York as commandant for Air France and in La Turbie where he and his wife had a beautiful home overlooking Monaco and the Mediterranean. Our friendship flourished for fifty years until his death in the 1980s.

Another good friend, George Tremel, pro-American, who I believe, was the head of American Express in Paris, went to Vichy under orders from America and was "burned." He went to Spain, to Portugal and then openly with De Gaulle as an envoy, knowing all the European countries and speaking impeccable English, Spanish with an accent, Portuguese, Latin and German. As secretary of the Free French, I saw him arrive in

San José every three weeks until my departure for New York. He gave me some addresses in New York that became very important in my life, such as Pierre Bourdelle, son of the famous French sculptor. George became head of the French Tourist Bureau at Rockefeller Center. We saw one another often. Speaking with Gregory Thomas, a friend I met through Bourdelle, who worked with Tremel when Thomas was in charge of information in the Therian Peninsula, he said, "I can tell you that Tremel is a good Frenchman without fear, and like nobody else."

I was able to receive Pasteur Vallery Radot, young son of the great Pasteur. He was sent by De Gaulle to give a conference on the life in France. I was in charge of translating his French into Spanish. I learned at this conference that certain diseases had disappeared. The Germans had taken away fat, alcohol, pate, truffles and meat. The French were reduced to a diet and even lost weight. Wine had almost disappeared and they were doing well. They returned to the past.

Another interesting person, whom I helped as much as possible and with pleasure, was a general in charge of the health of French troops. I can't remember his name but I will never forget his personality. He came from Guiana and had the responsibility of seeing to the health of the prisoners there. Later De Gaulle sent him on a great mission of his own. It was impossible for the French in Costa Rica not to question him on the men condemned to confinement. He explained that he often heard the confessions of these men. All of them were not criminals like the French had heard. Poaching game for example is a defect of the French peasants. Those who had killed and escaped the guillotine in his view were no better or worse than many humans. In the hospital he had these same men as nurses and they did their job with conscience, as well as the career nurses. His assistant in the operating room had a usefulness that he did not know how to replace. And yet this same man was incapable of breaking his promise to kill an ex-accomplice who arrived in the penitentiary knowing that this man had rescued him. These are complicated stories. Perhaps life had been against him from the beginning.

I saw many kids in France, I would say born well, who were not able to survive in poverty. It is difficult to keep moral shame when poverty has been for their family a way of life. They didn't have backing from the example of their parents. I saw young girls leave their rags at the price of prostitution. For boys, intelligent boys, the pathway was outside of the law. Perhaps the general was right. These criminals were only a little bit different from normal people.

A memory from the time of Don León Cortés, a great period for me, was designing an altar for a chapel in a lepers' house near Tres Rios to be constructed by the Public Works under my direction. Spanish Sisters of Charity complained that they had to go very far to worship and receive communion. Dr. Rena Echeveria, minister of health, reassured me that there was no case of contagion. I was happy to do this for these brave women who were performing remarkable service and not thinking of financial reward. My designs have been respected but the scenes that I was hoping to sculpt in mahogany were given to a Spaniard not educated in art and that gave me certain problems. I was pleased to see it finished and to attend the dedication ceremony.

Echeveria then asked me to decorate his office in a new building being completed. I proposed using my students from school and working with Costa Rican wood of different colors. Before finishing the designs Echeveria was replaced by Alberto Cusma. It was he who gave me all the documentation to develop my idea that was to begin with the invention of the microscope and all the nations that fought disease with special attention to tropical diseases. This frieze of inlaid wood was interrupted with a large panel representing hygiene and the fighters who had died without a sign of their nationality. The students happily followed the tracing of my design with each color of wood. It was like a game for them. I designed the furniture in the office and the library in wood, parchment and forged iron.

A remarkable personage was Doña Maria Fernandez Tinoco, widow of Tinoco who tried to become dictator and expatriated to France. Her brother who was head of the army was killed in the revolution. After her husband's death, Madame Tinoco returned to Costa Rica and worked at the museum of San José. I visited the museum and met her there. This was prior to holding my classes. She spoke French well and helped me to advance my Spanish. We established a great friendship. I found her a person of good character, extremely intelligent, cultured and busy with art generally. One day I received the order for a portrait of her late father, Don Mario Fernandez, founder of the College of Señoritas. The director of the college and the government entrusted me with enough pictures. I decided out of personal pride to execute the work by hammer from a piece of half-red copper, a surface of 70 by 80 meters and 8/10ths of a meter thick, and to give it form without soldering. I envisioned not only a likeness of a great man, but a work of art. At this time I would have carved a mountain if anyone asked me to. Then one day I got my courage to ask Doña Maria to come and give me her opinion of the portrait.

She arrived well dressed and as always wearing a hat. She reminded me of true French women of her age. We embraced. Then I showed my work to her. In a forthright way she said, "Louis, it's magnificent but my father had two depressions, one on each temple." She took off her hat and revealed the same depressions on her temples that her father had which were not apparent in the pictures.

"Oh, that's nothing." I said. My metal was annealed and ready to be worked. I chose my hammer and gave the necessary strikes to make the depressions.

She called out, "That's it, that is my father. Louis, it's perfect." I didn't touch it any more. It was installed at the College for Señoritas following an inauguration with authorities represented including Fisseux. Leslie, my wife, so dear, thinks the sculpture Don Mauro Fernandez to be my most beautiful portrait.

Madame Tinoco was the one who introduced me to pre-Columbian objects in ceramic, metal and stone to which she had dedicated a good part of her life. She presented me with a piece called *Maja* that had been given to her after her time in exile in Guatemala. It is an ornate vase with Mayan characters and in excellent condition.

Chapter 12

Tropical Expeditions

To become better acquainted with this beautiful country, I had the pleasure of taking several expeditions with Jacques Pigeonneau, chargé d'affaires at the French legation. He has always been a good companion. He asked me to make an eighteenth-century Regency tea and coffee service that I completed before he left Costa Rica. He parachuted into France during the occupation. He was very active, a great Frenchman.

Staying over at Puntarenas in the middle of music out of doors, I asked myself how couples could dance all night in the humid atmosphere and be able to simply live the day that follows. Having shared the baths with enormous toads, I felt a little bit refreshed after a sleepless night.

The captain was waiting for us at the jetty. He said that it was necessary to leave right away because of the tide. The boat did not inspire confidence but we put in our bags and arms and followed a route for Puertro Nil, I believe in Guanacaste. His money received, the captain didn't lose any time. It was nighttime. We would not have been able to see friends at our departure as the jetty was in bad shape, missing planks all the way along. At dawn there was a rancho visible in the distance.

The inhabitants who live by fishing and little gardens hid themselves. Prudently, we transported our baggage and after a while they showed up, fearful but not hostile. We learned that our horses were here but were taken away and would be returned later. Meanwhile we stayed to chase crocodiles, which amused the people. In the afternoon we had our horses and guide who helped to arrange our baggage on each horse. These poor creatures were badly cared for, their ears down—a sign of vampires. After goodbyes we set off to cross the Cordillera with the intent to arrive before nightfall. In the beginning everything was going perfectly. We stopped to drink a warm Coca-Cola. Then we crossed the jungle. Because of the vegetation the visibility was not good and by 5:00 or 6:00 p.m. it was very black. On route we went down a hill. A cowboy said to me, keep the head of your horse high and let him choose; he sees better at night than you do.

At the bottom of the hill we saw a vague light and stopped to discuss it. The guide wanted to continue but we disagreed. In the middle of the forest we arrived at a clearing with about ten ranchos. The village seemed abandoned except for a fire in the interior of one of them. There was an old Indian woman cooking and that was the light we had seen from afar. As her Spanish was not too bad we said that we were dying of hunger. She offered us pieces of filet of puma with corn, also black bean soup with an egg floating in it. This is a meal I have remembered. And then the villagers returned who had been waiting for the old woman to investigate the visitors. They were like ancient people. It was remarkable.

This was my first trip on a horse since my military service and after twelve to fourteen hours of travelling I couldn't wait to wash up. I spoke of it with my companions and asked an Indian boy where I could bathe. The answer was—the stream. I saw my friends copy me. They were not in good shape either. We then asked where we could spend the night—at the school. All of us were content; we were exhausted and in no time there was silence. Awakened by the sun in the morning, to our surprise, the school was a school but it wasn't completed and had no roof. Everybody was in tears of laughter to the amusement of the Indians who were watching us shave. And then friendship and a little breakfast with egg tortillas. Everything was delicious.

We learned that we were two hours by horseback from Liberia, the capital of Guanacaste and continued our vacation in this part of

Costa Rica where I was always happy: Nicoya, Santa Cruz, Feladelfia and Baya, these areas.

Another time, invited to Finea El Tenorio, we arrived at a little part on a river where a guide waited for us with horses. I realized that he was an Indian, an instructor, and spoke perfect Spanish. He had a joyful nature and we became friends. Bushes, identical bushes, surrounded our route in the middle of the Cito swamp. I understood why men lost their way risking their lives but our guide did not make a mistake. I traveled by his side, observing everything. We were separated at times but always in view of one another. Then he stopped me. He got off his horse, picked up a stone and threw it. A rabbit was hit on the head. He put it in his back pouch. After four hours on horseback we arrived at El Tenorio. We could see buildings and an alley of at least two hundred meters and a width of about one-kilometer opened up before us. The reception was friendly, but we were not invited to chase our fatigue, heat, thirst and weakness.

The proprietor invited me to hunt a puma that had killed several calves. It was the last hunt of my life and a hunt without risk because the puma was afraid of dogs that abused him with noise, so much so that he took refuge in a tree where the only danger is to be killed. He was wounded and without fear. The foreman of cowboys said to shoot him in the flank and he would shoot him in the head. The poor beast fell and all of this for absolutely no reason except for the calves that he had killed.

In the middle of the swamp a dog was fighting some sort of bear that had long deadly claws. Despite our calls he had given up. The cowboy and I went back to see the dog that lay wounded and bleeding. Without hesitation he had his lasso ready and prepared to drag the dog to the house. I protested, jumped off my horse, picked him up and carried him in front of me observing that his throat had not been touched.

I was upset to bring the dog back like that. The manager, a Spaniard from Cartago, brought me a disinfectant and I asked for a needle and thread to close up the sore. The dog in my hands almost without moving seemed to understand. The manager put him on the porch with bags beneath him. Only the guests had the right to go onto the porch of the main house. The employees and everyone I had seen on the property stopped and took off his hat. One of them asked to speak with the leader. The dog got better with the care of the two of us. Then the same Indian friend asked to drive me to the boat at night before low tide. After twenty minutes or so he said, "Look, Louis, the dog follows us." He was not attached like the other dogs and perhaps he knew we had food. What was I to do? The boat would not wait for me. After fast words and gallops to the house with the dog we asked that he be enclosed or attached.

The Indian, I think his name was José, said to me quickly, there are four more hours of daylight. All was for the best. The boat, loaded, was in fact waiting for me. I pulled José to my chest and said goodbye, thanking him for being a friend and guide. The ocean was hard with water coming up the sides of the boat, which was too heavily charged. At daybreak we could see triangles on the water. I was the only one concerned.

There is another story that remains with me. At this same rancho the manager asked me where I had studied. My reply was that I followed the School of Art receiving lessons in design, *modelage* and anatomy. The employees of the farm were listening. Later the foreman of the cowboys asked him if I would be able to see his wife who was not feeling well. I answered that I was not a doctor and couldn't do anything. He had heard that I had taken courses in anatomy and that I must go to see his woman in their shack that was very near. I realized that she was suffering from malaria and was weak. They had four girls. I counseled him to have her rest and then to go as soon as possible to Liberia where there was a clinic and doctors. Later, I heard that he took her there and she had come back greatly improved after treatment.

At this same farm, I started to make a drawing of a young boy in pencil. Without a doubt the resemblance was good. The father who had not left us asked what I was going to do with the portrait of his son. Right there something said to me that he was frightened to see the portrait leave. For him I had become capable of changing the life of his boy. The fear of magic troubled him and tension was mounting, and so I offered it to the father who was reassured and he gave me many thanks. What did he do with the drawing? Does he still have it or did he destroy it? The man came from the central plateau, absolutely Spanish in origin.

Before this experience, I had a chance to realize how much the Costa Ricans were subject to superstition. A man at the Public Works treated me badly, he was jealous or something of no importance to me. Later on he was killed in an accident. Then, one of my managers at the school said to me, "Don Louis, I do not believe that I would want to be your enemy."

Before that, I was at the office of Public works in the middle of educated engineers. One of them, coming from Guanacaste where he had worked to build part of the Pan American road, recited a belief of the elderly in the camp where everybody lived. A woman appeared, coming from nowhere, and without asking permission took care of the kitchen and laundry to keep them clean. Someone did not pay her respect. According to the speaker she disappeared in a fog. Awkwardly I explained what I had heard regarding this belief. One engineer, educated in Europe, looked at me shocked, I would say incensed, with my story. It was this lesson that made me give up my sketch. I don't know what would have happened to me before taking off for Puntarenas. I had become superstitious too.

Pigeonneau, Reddy Hart, the driver and I had a unique experience. Having only one track, we had to wait for the ordinary train to pass on its return to Puntarenas. This was in the middle of nowhere. In Puntarenas we met another Belgian, Charles Lejeune, who earned his living hunting crocodiles in this part of the country and exporting their skins. He was married to an Indian girl who he met traveling by horseback from the United States to Costa Rica where he lived poorly. On our arrival we were invited for a meal. His wife told us what had happened several days before. The two of them were in a canoe with just an axe. He had a lamp on his forehead when he saw his lamp reflected into the eyes of a crocodile. She guided the canoe toward the animal. Lejeune hit him with the axe behind the head but missed killing him and he fell into the water. The woman took the axe from his hand, killed the crocodile, put the canoe back into place and with him brought the dead beast to land. This beautiful woman gave us the idea of being ready to die for her man. He was a captain in the Belgian army during World War I, but in spite of being educated in a university he was never able to adapt himself. What he missed was peace. He tried ever since to risk his skin.

Everyone spoke of Sandino who was a hero according to some people and a bandit to others. A witness was Lejeune, who had gone through all the countries of Central America. One late afternoon he found a *pasada* where he decided to spend the night. The owner advised a man, a German, not to leave that night. Lejeune listened, watching this man laugh, showing off his gold teeth. He left against the advice. The same night, some peasants began to provoke the gringos, brandishing their machetes on the ground, looking at the macho, ready to have the joy of refusal. Charles, who was not a bluffer, told us that he had seen armed types like these men terrorize the place. He asked for a machete and received one. He chose the one who seemed to be the most hostile of all and feigned the use of his machete. The other one, a little bit surprised, did not know what to do. Then, seeing that he would not be able to escape in front of everybody, he put himself on guard. Lejeune had been prepared to use his saber. He approached the man who was still surprised. He made a pass on the side of his head almost cuffing his ear and this to say that if he wanted to get killed just keep persisting. That was the end. The following day, en route with his wife, they found the body of the German killed with his face cut up to take out the gold teeth. His chest was cut open, what they called "Le corte cholero."

I learned later on that the guerillas don't always have a choice in their membership and their means of fighting. What is certain is that this story stays. I received several points of view from European people living under the dictator, Samoza. It was predictable that without the aid of the Americans, who felt the war was coming; it would not have lasted such a long time.

Another excursion was to Buenos Aires with Pigeonneau and Reddy Hart, a Belgian who took his name when he earned his living as a circus cowboy in the United States. He was a remarkable shot, good with a lasso and sang all the airs of the cowboys well. We visited Felix Zeiden, a naturalist, very Catholic, who was well-to-do enough to pay for an airplane to bring supplies and to have a priest come to celebrate the mass from time to time for himself and the Indians who loved him. At the Sabana airport we took off in a small plane. Our baggage was piled up in the middle of boxes of all sorts. The mixture was unbelievable, including chickens that were just born destined for lost people absolutely without airplanes. We reached Isiorodel, a half hour from San José. This same trip by horseback would take fifteen days going over a chain of mountains, El Cerre de la Muerto (sadly named), leaving a lot to chance. Too many men have left their skins there. There wasn't any reason to take the risk. I don't want to bluff, but perhaps with other people I would have tried it. It was at the time when I wanted to prove myself to myself.

In the plane we asked the pilot, "Where are the seats?" Startled by the question he looked at the other passengers. Some peasants sat on the floor or on boxes and were clearly not used to it. They laughed and we did the same. On route, obtaining the peak of the chain of mountains in the south we saw another one in the north that had a plateau where San José is well situated and protected. I felt doubtful as the plane almost touched the tops of the trees. The pilot assured me that we would stay above the branches. Then suddenly I could see two large landslides at the bottom of a valley in the distance looking like a road touching the forest. There was a big descent. The road that I had seen from the plane was the airport. I admired the ability of the pilot to land there. He seemed completely sure of himself and the plane. A guard with horses and a telegram from the president was waiting for us. He was young, about thirty, without a gram of fat, strong, intelligent-looking and friendly with intense black eyes. During the trip he did everything he could to protect us and keep us happy.

The horses were ready and the bags attached. Not sure of the water, we had whiskey and coffee because that had to be boiled. We had the guides bring along purchases for the people we would visit during our stops. To get out of the valley we had to pass the course of water, Le Goneral, fifteen times, sometimes counting only on the instinct of the horses to arrive at the other side. We crossed our legs not to get too wet, also sitting with our weapons across our laps and praying to God in the crossing. My horse lost his footing for I would say ten meters. I was not proud but holding him well we ended up reaching the edge where my companions were apprehensively waiting for me.

Toward night the guard advised stopping at a rancho where a white man lived absolutely alone, and instinctively arrived where he needed to arrive. The owner of the rancho grew tobacco for himself and to sell in order to buy weapons, medicine, matches and whatever he needed. He was a dentist from San José. One day he decided to go onto the land alone. He seemed happy with our visit. The mosquitoes and other insects the horses attracted were like nothing I had ever seen before. The single light was an electric torch. Pigeonneau had the bad idea to open a box of conserves that he received by diplomatic valise. It produced an explosion in the heat, making us laugh for a moment. We were served pâté with truffles a little warm but delicious, giving an air of a big feast in the middle of a part of the world, unknown and isolated and appreciated by the four of us.

Our host rolled his cigars that he smoked to get rid of the flies and mosquitoes. He rolled one for me. I commented on the good tobacco and he was pleased. At our departure the following day he gave me a package of cigars of his in a beautiful package of tobacco leaves. "Abazar and God accompany you," he said. We thanked him for everything.

Our horses clean and nourished, we took the trail again. Sometimes our guide went ahead by foot to reassure himself that he was on the right path. He explained that the vegetation was so thick, in three months the path would completely disappear. After the day's journey it was arranged that we stay at a farm of an American married or not to a half-Indian girl. They had three children. There was a clearing shared by the joining of two rivers, a superb place that gave them fishing, hunting and a big garden.

This American had been gassed in the war in France and believed that he was condemned. He came to Costa Rica with a pension and now seemed to be cured. He received us effusively, delighted to speak English with Pigeonneau, but especially with Reddy. He also spoke Spanish well and was familiar with the Indian language. The place was beautiful and the hospitality so good we stayed several days despite the demands of our guide.

The next morning, our weapons ready, we followed the young Indian guide. The day passed when suddenly he froze, his ear extended and said a jaguar heard us. He left, forcing us to go back without anything. We were walking in a line when the Indian barred the road and without a word showed me a snake ready to attack. Whispering, he asked me to shoot it. We were only ten feet at the most. I aimed at its head, shot, and it fell to the ground. Everyone got back together, but the Indian and the guide stopped us. They did not want to move. We asked why. They didn't see the head. They knew that this snake, Mano de Piedra, doesn't pardon, even dead. Everyone remained immobile for I don't know how long. The Indian was barefoot, but the guard was dressed like we were. He began to look for the head that had the poison. The danger was not only for us but also for a passerby. The poison lasts almost one year.

After about an hour, the guard asked me if I wanted the skin, Yes, I answered. He reached for his hunting knife. Then he took hold of the snake, opened up the middle of the stomach, emptied him the best he could and still with his knife put him opened up on the trunk of a tree at eye level with the intent of cleaning him. Suddenly, looking just above the knife he saw the head of the snake with fangs implanted in the bark of the tree. With this same machete he dug a good hole next to the path, took the head on the point of his machete, placed it carefully in the hole, covered it well and cleaned his weapon thoroughly. Then he cleaned the skin, rolled it and handed it to me. At the rancho, he filled it with salt until I could have it tanned in San José. On our return the mistress made superb boullion.

Once more we were en route and finally to the place of Felix Zeiden, which was our destination. Zeiden was Syrian, very Catholic with a need to convert and protect the Indians who loved him. He was well to do enough to pay for an airplane to bring supplies and had a priest come from time to time to celebrate mass for himself and the Indians. He had a store where he sold everything people needed in exchange for products excavated or produced by the Indians. He received us like the lord of the manor. His servants prepared dinner. He surprised us by serving good French wine that was appreciated after a long and difficult trip. Later in the evening I was invited to take part in a game of lotto with Felix and some of his Indian friends. After a while I had all the pegs and I had to play very late in order to lose my gain before I could get into my hammock. No room had been left for me, however I found a bench that was long enough and just about large enough. I was so tired that I said to myself, don't move. I crossed my arms and fell asleep until morning, awakened by voices questioning how I did that.

After a marvelous breakfast, Felix arranged an excursion with his best horses. Clearly he was the chief of the village; very humane, intelligent, full of good sense and not wishing to lose the influence he had over the people who were the source of his business. He sent back to San José utensils and other objects; Indian gold work and weapons, but especially pre-Columbian gold objects.

An Indian who had played cards the night before, the school master, who was not Indian, Pigeonneau, Reddy and I set out the next morning observing the countryside change from forest to the savanna swamp. I don't remember passing a waterway or a single habitation but felt that we were not alone. During these excursions I often experienced this sensation.

We arrived at a place immaculately clean, a change from locations of non-Indians who did not care about their surroundings. No inhabitants were present. To my surprise the schoolmaster said they observed us before we entered the village. Getting off our horses, very gently, a master approached and invited us to enter. We were presented to the chief of the Indian group. It is difficult to say his age, perhaps forty or forty-five. He was small in the legs, but large in the shoulders, giving an idea of extraordinary power. One thing that struck me, he had eyes that crossed. He was dressed in impeccable white, barefoot and proud. He spoke Spanish and exchanged a few words with us. I noted that only one female was introduced, a very old woman taking care of the fire and the house. He seemed to pay no attention to her. Moments later, in Indian file as always, the people came out of the forest that surrounded the village, first the men, then the little kids and after the women, one of them was very beautiful. She was so pregnant one wondered how she could walk. We were surprised when the chief said that the little tribe was on a visit to Talamanca. I respected their right to say what pleased them. The memory of the conquest was still present.

Then there was a good union between all, the young and the old together. Reddy amused everyone with his circus tricks and lasso and stopping a horse in course only with his tail. He said later that when the horse feels himself grabbed by the tail, he stops. An exhibition of shooting followed. Reddy placed a little box of matches on top of a stone and with a revolver at one hundred meters made it roll. They admired him but were a little fearful. At Reddy's request I fired a shot with my carbine rifle and rolled over the little box. Then the Indian chief came to my side. The box was still on the rock. He showed me his peashooter almost two meters long made of bamboo with a little wax at the end similar to what they have at the end of a rifle butt. He took clay and wet it with saliva, rolled it in his hands and put it in his mouth, raised his weapon and blew—a bull's-eye shot. To think of the superiority of our firearms, to have acceded to the invitation of a man of the circus, and to have shown my capacity with a gun (something I have never been proud of), all of this is to my shame. More than fifty years later I can still feel the sensation of my embarrassment. And why does one learn to kill without the excuse of survival?

Openly, however, I admitted my admiration, particularly to the Indian chief with the crossed eyes. I learned that they were never afraid of hunting puma. Several of them bombarded the animal from all sides using pieces of wax. The blow to the head made the puma lose his equilibrium. Without giving him time to get up, they killed him with their machetes, which are indispensable in every phase of the chase. They hunted birds, monkey, deer, in fact everything necessary in their primitive life. We were offered food, but the memory of the old woman spitting into it made me refuse.

Without the airplane, we would need fifteen days in order to have the pleasure of spending several hours in the company of these Indians who were living almost like their ancestors before the conquest. I have often asked myself what the Spanish people have done to the Indians. Then I read that on their arrival to Costa Rica, they did not find anyone to enslave and that is why the Spaniards rolled back their sleeves and did what was necessary to survive. The Costa Ricans are still proud and respected in Central America, much more than other peoples I have met.

After the lesson of humility, we returned to Felix. He was happy that we found friendship with his friends, who counted so much in his way of life. They obtained objects asked for by the museums. In parenthesis, one night I asked Felix if he had some Indian things in gold, and he showed me several pieces. Attracted by a small figure lightweight as in filigree I asked him the price. I did not have much money with me, but without this excuse I found his price high. He made me think of the Arab rug merchants with their merchandise laid-out in Paris. Felix was very humane, intelligent, full of good sense and not wishing to lose the influence he had over the people who were the source of his "business," but as a merchant, Louis found his pricing high and Felix inflexible. Louis made a purchase. He may have misjudged Felix. Felix sensed Louis' thought and excused him. I paid him and still have the pleasure of this little piece in our collection and the memory of a good friend. We then returned to San José, and I was to take up again the work that was waiting for me.

I had in my studio a companion, Modesto, who was tired of the tranquil life in San José and was agitated by a group of men who came to sell me some nuggets of gold. The sum total of what they received was more than Modesto earned in a month. He did not know how much time they had spent and the risks and dangers they lived through. One day he announced that he would join the gold-seekers. They were all in the south and each designated a site on the river. They took their chances. I never wanted to visit these places infested with malaria and crime and I knew from the same men that the only one who flourished was the Chinese merchant who sold them tools and products they needed. They paid with what they took from the water, after spending hours and hours in the torrents exposing themselves to parasites and worms in the body that I believe attacked the intestines. I was going to dissuade him, but he didn't wait. On his return, Modesto had enough money to console himself. He told me his story.

The men were looking for a sheltered spot where gold would accumulate despite the current. It was these riches that all of the companions naturally hoped to have. They were well dispersed, aware of the danger of being robbed or killed for one's gold. It became an obsession. Fear dominated this part of the river. Needless to say, there were no police. Police sent in the past had become contaminated by gold fever and joined them. Modesto believed himself to be slyer and decided to leave. He was rather happy to possess a small fortune that he wasn't ready to share. Like all the others in this climate, he wore only pants. He pretended that he was going to see the Chinese man, filled up his pockets with nuggets and put himself in the water with the intention to cross drifting down. Forgetting that gold is extremely heavy; he gave up to the river a big part of his treasure so that he wouldn't drown. He should have known that, working as an *orfèvre*. Then he was not able to get to the other side without being attacked, so he came back to San José. I don't know what became of Modesto. I never saw him again.

I had among my clientele almost the entire colony of Venezuelans who had left their country after the death of the dictator Matute Gomez. This colony gave me opportunities to make sculptures in wood, *orfèvrerie*, jewelry and medals. They truly appreciated my work and often thanked me with a reception after an installation of a piece.

One of them, upon receiving a large nugget as a gift from the ambassador of Venezuela to Costa Rica, had the idea of returning it to him embellished. He asked my advice. I proposed mounting it on silver, creating an environment where the nugget was found including little rocks and vegetation where excavation was impossible. Inspired by my astonishment with his nugget and ignited with my idea, he told me these stories.

As a new governor of the region, the officials of this province had received him in the house of the ex-governor. There were two long banquet tables. In place of dishes was a succession of gold nuggets. He told me that he had never seen so much in his life. Another time he saw a nugget holding a door to keep it open.

An Indian coming to a village to sell his products spotted a mass of gold shining in the sun. He couldn't resist. He went down to the edge of a stream. He filled his *alfoyas*, a piece with double pockets, one on either side of the horse indispensable for people traveling on horseback. Then he couldn't lift them or bring them up to the road. He arrived at a decision and was found dead with his saddlebags filled with gold.

Another trip was to the banana region. Pierre Ducuron, secretary of the French legation, was following the interests of his wife as head of a plantation. He made visits to see how the bananas and coca were thriving. Always ready to travel, I accepted the invitation of this dear friend. Henri Schwan, Dedi as he was called, came with us. He was my former brother-in-law to whom I taught my trade. Benedetti also joined us. I was astonished by the trip to Port Limon, stopping at Siguirres, the most beautiful part of our travels. The manager of the farm was waiting for us. With the help of peons, he took care of our bags and all things useful for the employees of the farm. Pierre came to Costa Rica very young; I believe at age seven or eight. His parents wanted to settle there. Then Pierre rented with an uncle. No one knew that he was French and he was accepted as one of them. This was very important for relations with the natives of the area.

All aboard a little train to see the farm and to receive the harvest, we installed ourselves the best way possible. The trip was short. At one point we had to take an auto train, this one drawn by mules. It was really interesting to observe these animals trotting along on the right side of the road, rarely in the middle where the crossings did not please them. Coming back toward Siguirres, we arrived at the house or office where the manager lived with his family, built on a knoll not high but high enough to see a river which I believe was called El Raventosos Chirripo. I would say a river very big and deep and filled with crocodiles, which were out bathing in the sun waiting for an error. To warn us, Pierre told a story of a Frenchman whose widow and daughter live in San José. This sportsman was impatient to wait for the boat that was to take him to the other side of the river. He walked into the river. That was the end. The crocodiles squeezed their victim and placed him in a hole until decomposition permitted them to nourish themselves. No one had doubt of the story; however, the people went fishing. We ate some delicious shrimp that made me think of lobsters. Benedetti, who was from Cartago, had the bad idea to make a mayonnaise sauce. Two people were indisposed during the night. It is better not to do that in the tropics and even less in the banana zone. Pierre and I touched it just to taste.

So many times I have confirmed my admiration for the natives of the places where I visited. On a little mule train passing over a bridge, Benedetti, who liked to hunt with a rifle, noticed a fish shining in the sun. He asked to stop the wagon and ran to the bridge. There was accompanying us an Indian who followed him and so did we. Benedetti aimed at the fish and missed him. The Indian, who had his arrow ready, shot and put his arrow right in the middle of the fish, having compensated for the refraction of light. Without hesitation, he threw himself into the water. The fish measured thirty feet. The bullet of Benedetti had damaged but not killed it. Within the law given to the Indian, he was happy and wrapped him in palms.

We completed several promenades, which for Pierre, the manager and the employees were the tours that had to be made every six months. For me, these tours were rich with learning. There were trees of all sorts, including mahogany easily four yards in diameter. Others lost themselves in the sky. The bases extended on a diameter of at least fifteen to twenty yards, forming deep wedges. I also realized that these parts had only been seen in the last twenty-five years. Before that these forests were visited for the *caoutechouc*, the rubber tree which was important to the Americans. Their culture was abandoned and transformed into a region for bananas.

The reason for having an Indian with us during this excursion was that Benedetti and some employees had gone the night before to hunt tapir, wild boar. They had killed one but under advice of the men of the farm left it until morning. Neighbors had understood that Indians were going to claim it for themselves. Before the Indians began to claim it there was nothing to say. It appeared that only the liver was good. However, he invited us to pay them a visit so that we would participate in the feast.

After continuing, we arrived at a river where there was a dugout canoe. It was one they had made from the trunk of a tree using fire to hollow out the interior. While admiring their competence, I was not very reassured because once inside there wasn't much chance to move without putting our lives in danger, especially knowing that the river was full of crocodiles. Everything went well and we arrived at the village where everybody was busy cutting the meat into narrow strips to hang above the fire to prevent decomposition. That is all that I remember, as there was no contact really.

Visiting another part of the farm we crossed some muddy land. Passing under a tree that had fallen, I slid and to save myself I extended my hand. In extreme pain, I let out a cry. The manager retraced his steps and with a machette cleaned a circle around me of at least five or six meters. Then he came back close to me, saying snakes don't go away after having bitten, so it is not that. "Look," he said, "you now have a bump. It was a big 'bala' ant that bit you." He said to me also that he looked for the thing, because if it had been a snake it would have been indispensable to know it in order to give me the antidote. Thank you to this brave man.

The farm was never calm. One afternoon, several of us were together when a rabbit or a hare was saving itself from a snake at least two meters long. No one moved. Without a doubt this was normal for them. I learned that men tolerate certain snakes that are not dangerous in order to keep rats or mice out of the house. I had never heard of a snake that could catch a hare on the run. I had my doubts. He told me that certain snakes hypnotize their victims that consequently lose their means of defense.

To return to San José by Siguirres, we walked just to the train station without pushing ourselves. All was well until Dedi, who was playing with a small branch, called out to make us see a pretty little snake that he had found. It was one of the most dangerous of snakes, a coral snake, very small, red and lethal. Everybody ran. The manager violently pushed Dedi aside, cut the snake in two and buried it without a word. I believe he thought the visitors brought only problems. As for me, I was happy to return to San José. I remember hearing that Costa Rica had the greatest number of snakes per area of any place in America. I believe it, for the stories on the subject of snakes go on endlessly.

Chapter 13

New York

In 1940, during a visit with Don León Cortés in the palace, he asked me why I had not become a naturalized citizen of Costa Rica. He was saying to me that I was appreciated and loved (his thought) and that he was sure that I would be elected to an office. The United Fruit Company had abandoned the Atlantic coast with the excuse that disease was affecting the bananas. With the idea of deciding for me, he offered me many acres of land from the national forest that was going to be distributed to national citizens only. The United Fruit Company would take care of clearing and planting and furnish a contract for harvesting, a nice present for partisans. I did not know how to get out of this manipulation of esteem and confidence, but decided the nicest way was to refuse. After thanking him I said that I could not forsake my country. I had my objections but could not forget the culture I received or made myself in France. I referred especially to my wonderful métier. Observing his face so tense in disappointment, I asked him, "In my place, in war, with one's county occupied, would you be able to change your nationality?"

He replied, "Louis, one does not abandon his mother when she's down."

At the barbers having a haircut, I heard the voice of George Lyons. Although he was quite a bit younger than I was we looked alike and were taken for brothers. In French, that he spoke perfectly, he said that he was leaving that night for Panama and would return to England.

One day I got a telephone call from Nelson Rockefeller, who was undersecretary of Latin American affairs and visiting San José. It was in 1943. He said that he was interested in what he had seen of my work. With pleasure I received him in my studio. He came with the director of *The March of Time*, Sam Bryant, and a French comrade from the *Times* working in Costa Rica. Rockefeller was very surprised that an artist of my qualities was living and working in this little country and proposed that I go to the United States. I answered that the United States was unsympathetic to followers of De Gaulle. He responded that the United States did not like De Gaulle very much but liked De Gaullists and that if I were interested to go, he would be able to help me. I had heard these same words before. Turning to Sam Bryant, he suggested that Sam be my sponsor and asked me to provide the name of a friend in the States. I agreed. Shortly after, to my surprise, I received papers to be filled out from the American embassy in order to obtain a visa to the States.

Rockefeller asked if I had other sculptures in my home. I telephoned Marguerite, who was happy to receive him. He admired my direct carving in granite of an Indian woman from Nicaragua. He looked at my collection of pre-Columbian gold and accepted a small eagle that Marguerite offered him.

Asking where he learned such good French, he said that he lived in France as a young student and with an allowance of five francs a week had enjoyed traveling around France on his bicycle. Later, his representative at the embassy came to the house and asked me how much I wanted for the granite head of the Indian woman. I answered the truth that it was not for sale. Refusing to take no for an answer, he returned several times saying that Nelson insisted—adding, you know, he is very rich and can pay your price. Months passed, and finally, giving in to demands, I offered it as a gift and "she" left. Then I received from Rockefeller an antique weather vane.

On the front page of the magazine section, the *New York Times* ran a picture of Rockefeller next to my sculpture with a caption stating that he bought the Indian head in Nicaragua, and with no credit to the artist. I was enraged. Sam Bryant demanded a correction. The secretary said that it was a mistake. No correction was made.

I arrived in Miami, Florida, just after a storm had half destroyed it. The palm trees were flat. No airplanes could leave for New York. On my flight from Costa Rica, I had met an official of the United Fruit Company who also needed transportation to New York. He was unbelievably helpful to me. He spoke no English but got my train ticket and sent a telegram to notify my friends who were waiting for me. The immigration service was courteous and the officer said that I was lucky. One day more and my visa would have terminated.

After a long train trip, despite my affection for trains, I was tired. Peggy and her husband, Willey Gresser, met me at the station and I was happy for friendship and memories. They drove me to the apartment that Sam Bryant had rented for me near his office at *The March of Time*. Sam introduced me to Dick de Rochemont, who, like everybody who knew him, was pro-French. Sam remained one of my best and most faithful friends. He was a writer and movie director. We frequently had lunch together. Much later, when I was established at Fifty-fourth Street with clients, Sam said, "Louis, we bought the house." He explained that when he signed to get my visa, he and his wife, Betty, decided to postpone purchasing a house to avoid the expense of the mortgage until I was settled. Not only did he sign his name to get my visa; he demonstrated an obligation to sustain the person he recommended—what a morality! Still today, after more than forty years of constant affection, this memory touches me profoundly.

The Gressers gave me precious assistance. The cream of intelligence came to their soirees where I met teachers from the university speaking French, for the most part, perfectly. It gave me an idea of what my life could be if fate had decided to send me into these places of study. I must say that Peggy was the center of these reunions. She had studied Oriental languages, Egyptian hieroglyphics, Latin, Greek, old and new French. That is what attracted her to speak with me on the Petain, I, who only spoke French. Her grandfather taught Oriental languages at Harvard. Wiley Gresser became a true friend. We went to symphonies together and attended many social events. Every Sunday, the Gressers invited me to their table. Willey introduced me to his accountant and recommended that I deposit my small fortune at Morgan Guarantee Trust, but later I was informed by the bank to close my small account.

I paid a visit to Rockefeller Center to thank Nelson Rockefeller for his assistance in getting my visa and he gave me a recommendation to Yard jewelers on Fifth Avenue. I was able to establish contact but, not speaking English, I called upon Esmerian for assistance. He was perhaps the best merchant of precious stones in New York speaking French and English and recommended that I promise nothing to Yard, that he had an office in the same building and that I should come to see him. I soon realized that Esmerian had put a banana peel under my feet. I had one other contact with Rockefeller but nothing came of it, as I was not yet a citizen of the United States.

Van Cleef & Arpels commissioned a design using the Egyptian sign representing wishes of happiness. At lunch, speaking with Peggy about it, and without hesitation, she wrote the sign on the menu. I thought that she would need to research. Peggy learned to play chess with an American master. In two or three years she was the American champion and later world champion. Thanks to her interest and capacity to play chess, I met Marcel Duchamp. Marcel and I were born in the same town of Rouen. We became good friends and I made his portrait in bronze which is in the Museum of Modern Art in Paris—well received by the director of the Beaux Arts, but without one penny, despite the fact that I was asked to do it. I made one casting of this portrait in terra cotta that I kept in my New York studio.

Duchamp was sparkling with intelligence and spirit. He was a friend of Bourdelle and we formed a trio completely in unison. The three of us had lunches on Twelfth Street near his residence. I would have had a model example of his portfolio that he offered to me, but it was too late. Time went by after his marriages and his marriages changed him, and finally, I didn't believe him. He was too critical of everything, but what a personality.

In April of 1946, I was given the hospitality of Rubel of Rubel Jewelry Inc. on Fifth Avenue. We agreed that I would make pieces for him including several chased boxes representing artists of the eighteenth century, and that I could do work on my own account in his studio. Rubel made me promise not to work for Van Cleef & Arpels. The milieu in this workshop was not interesting, and there were cheaters from the foreman to the sweepers. Many of his employees were Frenchmen and some Germans, one of whom was a box-maker and we became friendly. Rubel called me Mr. Artist.

Then one day, a part that Dedi was finishing left me time to begin a dancer. The foreman came to my bench accusing me of lacking conscience. He had made a dancer for Van Cleef in Paris, and he didn't want any other person to do another one. I responded that I had never seen it; that what I was beginning was my idea. He insisted about our arrangement and my word. It was enough for me. After finishing the work we were doing for Rubel, I asked Dedi to collect our tools and pack the bag. We left. At the bottom of the staircase, I looked in my small address book for the next recommendation—Pierre Bourdelle.

I was convinced that the son of such a sculptor would be impossible, however, I reasoned it out, and decided that he would be able to advise me. His studio was two blocks from Rubel. Pierre was a man of general culture, an artistic culture, difficult to match. Without detours we became friends and later on like brothers. I explained my difficulty in finding studio space to install myself. Without any hesitation, Pierre offered to share his studio. He was executing lacquer on linoleum to decorate the interior of a boat, I believe, *La Savanna*, formerly used to transport troops. I thanked him, but was certain that the presence of the flame that I needed would lead to histories of fire. He said, "Let me talk with the owner who has his business on this street."

On the same floor where Bourdelle was located, I rented and shared the space with a jeweler. We had one safe in common separated in two, sharing the cost of electric protection, which was indispensable in order to have the confidence of our clients. This man was intelligent and a superb jeweler, but with low morals. I would not have chosen him as a neighbor if I had known him beforehand. He committed several crimes, not only against me. Having the right to renovate, I had a partition built and a separate entrance made. I arrived at the decision that he must leave.

Orders came to me from Van Cleef & Arpels, Verdura and Kovan. I was confident but not at the end of my problems. Marguerite was not fully recovered from her operation. She asked me if I was planning to stay in New York, not realizing that funds were becoming rare, that it was not my character to abandon New York when I saw my chance to work and to survive there. Marguerite had become discouraged and negative about Costa Rica, making life difficult for me in San José, and I had accepted the offer of Rockefeller to help me to come to the US. Thus, I accompanied her to Miami, where she was going to join someone I did not know at this time.

Before my departure, Pierre Bourdelle had said to me that he was going to Miami and on the return would be in Newport News, Virginia, where work was being done on his lacquered pieces. I could take a bus that would drive me to a naval chantier. I found the bus in question, went aboard, but the bus did not leave. Everybody looked at me. I didn't understand when the bus driver asked me something, as my English was inadequate. He took my luggage and by the shoulder pulled me toward the front of the bus. I had chosen the back because it was empty. Pierre was waiting for me. Speaking with the driver, he began to laugh. He translated to me what had happened. In 1946, the back of the bus was reserved for blacks. I had chosen it without meaning to protest against anything.

This over with, Pierre introduced me to the military authorities in charge of the naval *chantier*, and a nametag was pinned to my clothes, as I was still a foreigner in the US. We were happy to be together. I was able to help him finish the work of repair to the lacquered pieces damaged on the ship. Happy to see the ocean again, we crossed the estuary to take the train for New York, where we found Rosario, Pierre, the son, and Didi, who was employed at the workplace during my absence.

After my arrival, with a recommendation from the Costa Rican ambassador, I paid a visit to M. Pierre Cartier, the proprietor of the New York Co., who received me nicely. He would be happy if I wanted to begin at the bottom and eventually to execute pieces. A special place would be reserved for me in a department of his store. He presented me to his director, M. Edmund Foret, who said that he was enchanted having me join Cartier. I had embellished boxes for Cartier in Paris.

He showed me all parts of the business. In the studio, right away I felt the hostility of two men who were independent, but not able to find similar employment elsewhere. The other workers were rather curious. Returning to his office, Foret confided that in seeing pictures of my work, there was no one there with my qualities.

Before leaving, I was presented to Pierre Claudel, son of the famous ambassador of France, who from the first impression was a small, good man. What a difference with Foret who was authoritative and intelligent and knew the métier like few men that I have met. In my rapport with these industrial people of the jewelry business, Pierre Claudel and I were alone, the only ones. I said to him that I would be very happy in the future to have my pieces signed at their place. I realized immediately that this did not please him. That was all.

A little later, I received some orders from Foret, but I decided not to begin. Pierre Claudel had done his schooling with Bourdelle at Lysee Henri IV. They considered themselves friends. Foret was also an old friend of Bourdelle, but on a basis of appreciation and mutual merit. Pierre told me that I was going to spend the weekend at the Claudels, who had a piece of property on Long Island. I had met the wife, Marion, who was charming.

Claudel asked me for some designs and perhaps to do some religious medals. As a true friend, Bourdelle confided in me something that shocked him. Before departing, Claudel asked Bourdelle about me. How long would I be able to hold out according to my friends? Bourdelle, a proud man, was astonished. He was too noble to accept this and did not ask me to keep quiet. I sent back all the orders received and the components that I had left with Cartier. The same evening, I had the visit from Foret accompanied by his beautiful companion. After exchanging our reactions, he declared to me, "You are right, Féron. I am sad, for I had dreams that I would be able to realize, thanks to you. It's finished with that guy." I received another invitation to work at Cartier, but Foret did not remain in their services. He returned to France. We corresponded until his death in the south of France.

The designer from Cartier, who was a friend of mine from France, came to my studio to see me. He was certain that I was the only one who would do honor to his design for the principal piece in the Cartier

Centennial. There was a long discussion, restaurant, and good wine. In friendship, I accepted the job. At delivery, all of the people who saw it were happy. I believed that I had done good work and was happy too. As I was leaving, Pierre Claudel stopped me and asked when we would have peace. That was easy. I would be willing to work for them, but to sign my pieces if they were my designs. He responded, yes, I know, but it would be necessary to come here to do it. I preferred to work in my own studio, not to lose the customers I already had, and to keep my liberty.

The son-in-law of Tiffany had introduced me to Tiffany. He was a gentleman, a Sumerian, and one of the furnishers of precious stones. He said that he would be glad to see my work. At this time, I did not yet have my studio. We met in Oyster Bay near Bourdelle's house. Pierre and his third wife, Ruth, had two children, Stephanie, named after Pierre's mother, and a son, Pierre. They kept in contact and were like family for Leslie and me.

I remember the call from Ruth saying that Pierre was in the hospital with a heart attack. Pierre asked for me. Ruth met me at the train station and en route I requested information in order to speak with Pierre. Ruth replied, "Impossible, Louis, the doctor forbids it." Despite all of that, I was led to his bed. He was under an oxygen tent and smiled at me. I understood that it was not so serious. Pierre was tormented living above his means in Oyster Bay to please Ruth. He had become a teacher of art at NYU's Post College nearby, and was panic-stricken. Orders, with the deposit of money, were accumulating. He received a commission from the college and a deposit for silver, enough to fill up a hole, and his tension had mounted. Confidently, I lifted a corner of the tent, asking him, not about his health, but about the problem.

After offering him money, directly, he said to me, "Louis, go to my studio. You will see a maquette. I cannot do it. Finish it for me. Thank you, Louis." Not to tire him more, I asked Ruth to drive me to their house. It was in the disorder that I was used to with Pierre, but I found the necessary things and left for my studio to execute the order.

I don't remember if he stopped smoking. He had a powerful body and was the only one I have ever seen light up a cigarette with one already in his mouth. Ruth announced to me that Pierre was out of the oxygen tent, on the convalescent hallway, and reassured. Later, when the piece was finished, he was better. I reduced again my price to help him and his family and sent a letter with my bill asking Pierre to establish another price convenient to him and the college. Pierre wrote a letter saying that despite his illness he wished to make them the beneficiaries of my price. He confided to me that thanks to this gesture, he had been accorded the privileges of being insured with a pension. I was happy for him!

Ruth had an engineering degree and was scientifically ahead of me. Pierre loved science and had always researched finding extraordinary solutions. His aide, Rena, an Italian woman, coming from his house to Manhattan by train, told me that Pierre was not well. His client needed the plaque he was working on by a certain date for her play. What had become of it? Rena had a certain taste for art. The design was already chased in the linoleum, which served as the base of the plaque. I knew his technique. I sacrificed a day of my own orders, and pushed myself rigorously, as I love to work. The same evening the work was sized, ready to receive the lacquer that Rena was able to apply.

I will never change my feelings about him, but I understood that he was bothered by my speed of execution. He considered his technique a secret demanding days and days to achieve. Wanting to help him, but not lose too much of my own time, I had done it in one day of work.

When Pierre entered my studio and glanced at a sculpture of mine which he knew well, and refused to look at it again, I knew that I had achieved something good. He was very distracted to the impossible.

One day, he received an order from Miami for a sculpture in metal that my work suggested to him, and asked me to come to see it, knowing that I would not deceive him. It was interesting, absolutely like a game of planes and colors and I said that I liked it very much. He was not admitting that it was too big to pass through the doorway and confessed that he didn't even think about it. "What shall I do, Louis?"

"Cut it in half and assemble it over there," was my answer.

Often, he came to our apartment for the evening at Eighty-ninth Street where we would lose ourselves in dreams of art. Sometimes the emotion was such that the three of us were in tears or almost. Departing for Oyster Bay, he would take my raincoat by mistake, or my glasses. Leslie was laughing and we all embraced happily. I must say that I never had such a friend. We were like brothers of the same blood, a brother that I had chosen.

Pierre introduced me to Gregory Thomas, who became a friend almost like Pierre. He was more than six feet tall, heavyset and wealthy. He lived alone on Fifty-fifth Street in an apartment with an enormous library. Gregory was well educated with degrees from Oxford, the Sorbonne, Cornell, Salamanca, and two or three other universities. He was an American and could be taken for an Englishman, a Frenchman, or a Spaniard, and also spoke Latin, Greek, Portuguese and Italian. During the First World War he was a student traveling, perhaps giving information to his country. He was in charge of intelligence for Spain, where he had good friendships, especially with the Duke of Alba, who had been his companion during his studies at Salamanca. He became indispensable during the war. His memory was incredible. At his home, I saw him in the middle of a conversation, get up to take a book, open it to a page and confirm what he was discussing. He was a true living library.

I followed him almost everywhere to know my new country better. Having an official appointment in Washington, he invited me. I followed him into an office where he introduced me and said to me, "Louis, this is not going to last. It's better that you wait for me here." He was the chairman of Channel and became an international lawyer. We visited museums and historic places—what a guide. Not only cultivated like no other person, he was a gourmet and a great connoisseur of wines and was crowned Grand Senechal of Bordeau. He helped me to develop a liking and knowledge of wines. Each morning, on a tour of the state of New York, he read to me, or had me read a book in English that had references to the trip that we were going to undertake. He introduced me to Cornell and for the first time I had the pain of realizing what I had missed. In these beautiful gardens, there was tranquility and cleanliness for the development of beautiful and high thoughts. (I remember the happy pain after a visit to a Catholic University in Rome with this atmosphere of peace, of intellectual concentration—in the middle of murmurs of gentle running water and the silence of gardens.) I was happy to live among these young men for one day. We were invited to a luncheon with the Dean. After a month visiting his relatives and friends and the Finger Lakes, we returned to New York City.

At the University Club together, talking about a person, Gregory said to me, "You see, he doesn't have our preparation." By nature, refusing to present myself as someone I am not, I replied, "Aside from two years after primary school, I am in the same category." Surprised, he answered, "You are so different."

What afternoons Pierre, Gregory and I had together. Everything was a little bit Rabelaisian, the thread of thought, the friendship and the culture. Then Gregory met Geraldine of Czechoslovakian origin. She was young but not too young, rather pretty, not too much, without culture but mature. He seemed happy to attempt the impossible, to make her acceptable in his milieu. She did not change him. They retired to Tampa, Florida, where she had grown up in good health, active and without problems. Gregory remains one of those I am unable to forget. I thank fate or God for having me know such friends.

At that time, Henri Agnel renewed our friendship. He was a pilot for Air France. He and his wife had been missing things in France since the war, and he used my studio as a depot where he hoped to receive his purchases. We had lunch together or dined with Rosario and family.

Marcel Rebiere was part of our group when he was not making a film with Dick de Rochemont, a friend of everyone. Marcel amused us with his vulgar manners. Marcel was well educated but followed the Beaux-Arts in Paris. Before this last war, he became a cameraman and made several films. The war led him to the trenches where he was wounded in his right hand, losing fingers. No longer able to use a rifle, he left the service. At the time of the Russian Revolution, he was sent to Moscow with General Janis (I knew the son of Janis in Costa Rica) to advise the socialist government under Kerensky who wanted to continue the war.

Marcel often came to the studio. His wife, Rene, was a cheerful person, always ready to have a good time. Like my mother, she was a superb cook. They lived in Jamaica, Long Island, in a little house that seemed to be a copy of his house in Eaux, France. They met before the war. Rene lost her husband in the war and Marcel's wife died. Marcel and Rene had always liked each other and got married.

In 1947, I received a commission from Verdura for a chased hinged box composed of autumn leaves of 18-kt. gold. His taste was of a very high level. It was a *tour de force* because each leaf was made and soldered to the others to give the impression of the falling leaves of autumn.

He was Verdura, le duc, and a friend of Jean Schlumberger. One day, Nico Bongard said that he had seen this box and also my *Faune* clip of pearl, platinum, gold and diamonds for the Dutchess of Windsor. Dick de Rochemont, who knew Nico Bongard in the film industry, invited me to lunch with Jean and that is the moment the decision was made to work with Schlumberger and Bongard. I visited their jewelry store at Sixty-fourth Street between Fifth and Madison.

I learned from Rebiere that Bongard was the nephew of Lavin, a jeweler of high reputation in Paris. They had been associated in New York, and then abandoned the business to answer the call to join the army of De Gaulle in France, subsequently returning to New York to start up again. I was more open with Bongard. Schlumberger never felt at ease with me. Personally, they did not give me an impression of old and certain friendship. Jean was capricious. Nico, who was always ready to serve him was kept in the background, for Jean was a jealous person and thought only of himself.

After a loan exhibition of jewelry designed by Schlumberger at the Wildenstein Gallery in New York in 1961, including twenty-three pieces that I executed, Jean extended his hand to me, apologizing for the publicity referring to him as the Benvenuto Cellini of the twentieth century. He said that without me the exhibition would not have been possible. I answered, "But why did you come to this declaration?" He answered, "It is not I, it's Tiffany." I don't remember a single instance when Bongard was recognized for his efforts. He was the soul of this affair.

I had Dick on the phone. He asked if a lot of my money was tied up with them and I answered, "More than comfortable." They had success and I had provision. It was before Christmas. A rich woman, who was supporting them, pulled out her funds; she thought Jean was thinking of marrying someone else. I called Bongard who was cool saying they had nothing, I would have to wait. I never appreciated Christmas, it's personal, but I had worked, and Dedi worked like a crazy one at my side. He was sad not to be able to buy what he wanted for his family. I got heated up with Bongard to the point where he used a slang word showing me the door. I stopped the conversation.

The following morning, Jean, all sweet in asking me my news, could see that I was angry about not being paid and that I would not back down. He asked me to at least finish the key. I assured him that I would finish any works that I had begun. We were separated for one year. They ended up paying me *tout doucement,* and I didn't lose any money.

I developed a line that I had begun with a luxury store for men called Blackwell. Mr. Blackwell was a gentleman of good taste and, I believe, wealthy. From words that I never doubted, he loved my production. He encouraged me. The cufflinks I made for him were selling in his small boutique. He liked the period of French Empire and gave me documents for the belt buckles, cigarette boxes, little balls with medals in the empirical style. This was my life saving leap.

In 1959, I read in the papers that Étienne Decroux, an acquaintance I met in Paris before I left France in 1934, was giving a recital of mime at the Cricket Theater, south of Greenwich Village. I telephoned him and wished him the best. He sent me four tickets and I invited Marcel and his wife to join me. After the performance, I congratulated him. I had known Decroux as an actor in the theater of George Dillon. Decroux was twenty-five or -six years of age at the time. I was fascinated by his fixed ideas that he shared with a young magician, also attracted to the theater, where I met superior people of all kinds, authors, musicians and actors. It was a marvelous period for everybody. Paris was vibrating like a storm. Art schools succeeded. We were like a bullion of culture.

I learned that Decroux's studio was two or three blocks from mine. He invited me to watch rehearsals of his troupe. Often at night, after my work, I went to see them. He enjoyed local theater, giving him a chance to rejuvenate mime, which had gone out of style. I was interested in the theater, looking for relations that touched upon art. It was there that I met Leslie Snow, who as a dancer, wanted to learn mime. I became so attracted by his productions that I spoke about it with Dick de Rochemont, who asked me if I believed it would be worthwhile to make a film. With my affirmation, he invited me to take a chance with him. This was done and the film was made. Decroux was one of the angels, but entering my life where I was able to judge him, I arrived at the conclusion in accord with Rebiere, that he was an idiot with genius. Decroux abandoned the US when he saw the success of his pupil, Marcel Marceau, coming to America. Marceau knew how to adapt the ideas of Decroux to the theater and only depended upon himself and not on a troupe and the many problems involved.

In 1965, there was an exhibition of my pieces at Post College with Richard Lippold, a great artist. It was arranged that I speak with students in a studio beforehand. I must admit that I have never been strong in public speaking. Fortunately, I had brought sheets of metal and some hammers and soon abandoned words and demonstrated what I wanted to say. A sculpture teacher, who had been an art gallery director in NY, displayed my sculptures and goldsmith objects for me in a room that may have been the living room of this house, very Louis XV. The pieces by Lippold were alone in another room. The praise received from a knowledgeable and responsive audience made us feel that the exhibition was a success.

Another exhibition of my work was arranged for the Boston Museum of Fine Arts Museum School with Lippold in February of 1966. Bourdelle was the *soleil* of everything. He accused me of refusing publicity, which was somewhat true. A French sculptor, Morenon, a former student of Les Beaux-Arts in Paris, was a teacher at the Museum School. Female teachers, who had never been invited to exhibit there, openly resented my show. Photos of my work remitted to the school disappeared for months. Shortly afterwards, The Boston Museum of Fine Arts accepted in their permanent collection *Portrait of Jean* and *Bordeau Cup*, which had secured my title, Meilleur Ouvrier de France in 1933.

I had all kinds of orders from Van Cleef & Arpels. Maurice DuValet was a designer with this jewelry house and one of my best friends in the trade. He was Parisian coming from a neighborhood similar to mine. Despite his success in New York, he was unable to overcome his background. From his design I was asked to make a small box for Mademoiselle Lily Pons. Lakne was represented in the middle of vegetation and flowers full of diamonds and precious stones. What a success; Lily Pons was delighted, and Claude Arpels called me to say how happy he was. On my next visit, he repeated his pleasure. I proposed to do another. This class of box placed him alone at the top in New York. He responded, "Yes, but afterwards, Féron, I would depend upon you, since you are the only one able to do it. Do you understand?" Later on, Arpels asked DuValet to ask me to make boxes for them. The repartee with these merchants was complicated and Maurice was not a fighter. I said to Arpels, "I regret that you did not take a chance with me" and I no longer worked for them.

Before this period, I had made a religious ring for Van Cleef & Arpels. The size of the diamond let me know that this ring could only be for a bishop. Sometime after, I received a telephone call asking me to come to the office of Monsignor Sheen at the Center of the Propagation of the Faith. With joy I met Monsignor Sheen, who became for me not only a client, a protector and counselor, but a friend. He had received as a gift a lot of amethysts of beautiful quality. What could be done with them? The monsignor spoke French. He had been educated at Louvin, this to perfection. He had an unbelievable presence and even more a gift as an orator, sacred or not. I received his order and returned with two or three designs for a pectoral cross of 18-kt. gold with the robe of Christ draped over the arms of the cross set with his amethysts. It was a dream color and all was accepted and executed.

He was so elated by this, he asked me to sculpt a Virgin for a show on TV. I arrived later with three *maquettes*. He gathered the men and women who were the head of this organization and gently asked for the opinion of each one. A long discussion followed. He then recommended that it was time to go and pray in the chapel, leaving me alone in his office. On his return, he said, "This Virgin." It was the one I had made directly from a piece of mahogany. It occurred to him that a reproduction could be made in bronze and replicas in a less expensive material for sale. The profit would go to the society. We never signed any contract.

Louis Féron died March 28, 1998 at the age of 96 and seven months. I went to France to confirm the accuracy of names, dates and places, as he wrote his memoirs from memory without notes, and I found his material factual.

L.S.

Crown of Thorns Pectoral Cross, 1955, direct carving in 18 kt. gold with crown of thorn motif. In the center of the cross is a large star ruby surrounded by twelve diamonds. Nine rubies are set in the thorn motif along the cross. Length of the cross is 4 inches. The gold loop has open work. Length of gold loop is 3/8 inch. Made in N.Y., for Bishop Fulton J. Sheen, New York. *Collection of the Vatican.*

Crucifix, 1959, hammered silver chasse in repoussé. Height: 44 in. *Commissioned by Clair Booth Luce in memory of her daughter Ann. St. Ann Chapel, Palo Alto, California.*

Head of Christ, 1958, carved mahogany, in the round. Elongated features with long hair in curls along the back, a moustache and beard, and an expression of sadness. Signed on the lower portion of the neck: Louis Féron. Height: 20 in. including round marble base. *Private Collection.*

Homage, 1964, in memory of John F. Kennedy, a direct carving in Indiana limestone of Jacqueline Kennedy with their two young children. Height: 18 in. on a base of wood.

Monstrance, 1946, silver gilt hammered and chased in repoussé. A praying angel kneels on either side of a crystal cylinder holding the lunulla. Gothic open work, thorn branches, fleur de lis and medallions embellish the piece, surmounted by a celtic cross. Louis Féron's first monstrance and one of his earliest commissions in the United States. Height: 32 in. *Canterbury School, New Milford, Connecticut.*

Monstrance, 1956, made for St. John's Seminary in Detroit, Michigan.

Louis and Leslie in New Hampshire studio, 1965.

PART 3

A Voyage Remembered

Louis and Leslie in their studio in New Hampshire circa 1978.

Chapter 14

Leslie Snow's Reflection

*L*ouis Féron lived a long and productive life. To my knowledge, he lived longer than anyone else in his family. He was vigorous with a passion for work. He loved his trade and felt grateful to have learned it in France. Louis' attitude was positive and optimistic in spite of poverty and suffering during World War I.

Louis believed that what he learned at home was his education. What he learned in school was instruction. He felt fortunate enough to have had parents who emphasized the importance of having a clear conscience and a clean name. He was hungry to learn. Deprived of formal schooling beyond eighth grade, because his teachers went to the front, he learned to study alone. He looked up to anyone who could instruct him and listened carefully to older experienced craftsmen who knew their métier thoroughly and could guide him. In the 1920s they were becoming irreplaceable.

He understood that he must take care of his health, stay clear of political controversy and learn how to work well at his bench. He said to me, "The way you start a project is critical." He believed in routine;

it freed him. Louis learned early in France that to be free is the greatest state of being there is in life and that freedom begins with discipline. Within Louis there was no trace of poor me. I never once heard him fault his parents or bash his government. He developed a great power of presence to face his problems. Louis had a sense of humor and often thought of his work as play. With one exception, he never received a toy in his youth; he made his toys.

Louis was born in one of the most Catholic cities in France—Rouen, Normandy. The father, Ernest Nöel Féron, a journeyman in a textile mill, was an orator and gave speeches at the mill defending Dreyfus, a French army captain, an Alsatian Jew, who was accused of espionage and was condemned to die in 1894. After a tumultuous court case, Dreyfus was pardoned and finally rehabilitated in 1906. The event divided France into two camps, as Louis expressed it, and led to the separation of the church and state. The father lost his job at the mill, and each job he found after that was for less pay; it brought the family to poverty. They moved to Paris and the only apartment they were able to find for a family of ten, including a blind grandmother, had no running water and one toilet for two floors of families.

When World War I started in August of 1914, Louis was thirteen years old. His nourishment was inadequate and he had no medical care. In the United States, scars on his lungs appeared in X-rays during his first visit ever to a hospital and showed that he had survived tuberculosis in his youth in France and every tooth in his mouth needed to be removed and replaced. Damage to his nervous system slowly healed as he worked at his bench in an atmosphere of peace in New England. Louis' father lived with his wife in Rosny-Sur Seine, near Paris where he was mayor for eighteen years. He died in 1948.

Louis believed in action. He spoke French, Spanish and some English, but I only spoke English. We understood one another well with body-language and agreed that words often get in the way of understanding.

In 1962, after a three year courtship, Louis and I married in a church in Tolland, Connecticut, a community where my sister Elizabeth, her husband and their children lived. After the wedding, we returned to Manhattan. Louis was looking for the right location to execute a newly commissioned work, and we decided to visit my mother in the village of Snowville, Eaton, New Hampshire. Across the street, Louis observed a mid-sized barn built about 1850 by my great-grandfather, Edwin Snow. The barn was adjacent to Edwin's home, which tragically burned down in a winter fire in 1940.

The ground floor of the barn, thirty-five feet in length, twenty-two feet in width, has an eight foot ceiling. We purchased this barn from my father's brother, Conrad Edwin Snow and made it our home retaining its simplicity.

Louis was organized. I don't recall him losing or misplacing anything, and he made many of his tools. I borrowed a chisel once and neglected to return it promptly. He said to me, "Look, I work with my two hands; I can only go as fast as my two hands can go. When I reach for a tool, I want it to be there." Surrounded with life-threatening problems in Paris during World War I, Louis built strong working habits that freed him to create with speed and assurance. His mind and his feeling were united.

I asked Louis to come upstairs to see a painting in progress. Looking at this painting carefully he said "Yes, but—" and he criticized my procedure. Before starting to work on a new piece, Louis planned the order of activities needed. The art of the goldsmith-jeweler-sculptor, particularly as Louis practiced it, is different from the art of the fine arts painter, but they share a vital principal—*the mind and the feeling of the creator must be united*. Louis' example made a positive difference in the quality of my work.

During a party, conversation turned to a subject that I thought inappropriate at the dinner table. Louis responded, "Why are you stepping on my foot like that under the table?" Another evening with good friends, Louis went into the bathroom, and came out in pajamas and bathrobe. He circled the dinner table to say goodnight to each guest as he was ready to rest and prepare for work with steady hands at his bench the next morning. He disappeared into the bedroom, drew the curtain and went to sleep.

We were having our afternoon tea and Louis said, "Thanks God."

"Do you mean 'thank God'?" I asked, and he answered smiling, "You're cheap."

But we agreed that words have a tendency to divide. With the exception of great poetry, language usually refers to the outside world and not to one's inner life and spirit. We understood meaning, intent and emphasis better from gestures of our bodies than from words and this was true from the first day we met. Louis was aware of suffering in this world. He overcame incredible hardships in France, and as a young man, he learned to focus and to live in the present. Louis was sturdy, joyful, and grateful to be alive. He had lifetime friends and was tender with children and animals. Our courtship and marriage were significant years of my life. Louis was a free man. Months before he died, Louis said to me, "Thank God I have you."

Louis Féron with cup, hammers, and chisels, 1975, drawing by Leslie Snow.

Photo of Louis Féron at Plymouth State College after commencement services and the presentation of an honorary Degree of Doctor of Humane letters by President Harold E. Hyde and Dean John C. Foley to Mr. Louis Féron.

I value this picture of Louis. It was taken by my sister, Elizabeth at Plymouth State College (now Plymouth State University) on May 21, 1977, after commencement services and the presentation of an honorary degree of Doctor of Humane Letters by President Harold E. Hyde and Dean John C. Foley to Mr. Louis Féron, Snowville, New Hampshire.

The picture captures Louis' focus and his humanity. I can imagine the soul-searching thoughts he is having at the moment the picture was taken. Although first in his class in Rouen, Normandy, and in Paris, he was unable to pursue formal education beyond eighth grade because of family poverty and complex political forces in France occurring before, during, and after the first World War.

Poetry of Leslie Snow

SONG TO LOUIS

My soul's longing lifts and soars
To life's beginning
Where love and labor singing
Bring wholesome joy.

Steps so light in seeking
Through work and love achieving
An ordered life believing,
Two lions face to face
Are side by side.

This, a record of my love,
Of discipline and daring
Of unity and sharing, transcends
All breaths and sighs
Reveals then dies.

It started on a winter's night
A New York Loft, Eighth Avenue
Where mimes and actors too
With silent power
Performed a comedy.

Many, many days went by
Players met, rehearsed with care
An audience came to see, and so did
A sculptor, goldsmith, jeweler
Watching gingerly.

In June, with flowering trees in bloom,
The troupe of mimes made a film,
Directed by Étienne Decroux,
Who played in *Les Enfants Du Paradis*
And trained Marceau.

Comrades three produced the film:
The director of the March of Times,
A camera man and a craftsman
With a lion's mane,
Who waited in the wings.

Back stage, when filming done,
There was a knock upon the door.
I opened. There he stood.
Neither spoke the other's tongue
We mimed instead.

He sat beside my dressing table
Jars of make-up lines a cloth,
And on the cloth he drew a ring.
Not knowing what this meant
My eyes withdrew.

Later, I wished that I had
Kept the little sketch. He invited me
To a small café with French cuisine
Earnestly we tried to speak, but failing
Turned to mime.

And so it went for days and months
Through winter, spring and summer.
Language skills improved, and slowly,
Deeply, we fell in love for life
With one another.

AFTERNOON

Together we shall have our tea
Beneath this graceful linden tree
With leaves of hearts that shimmer
In a summer breeze
A breeze that filters sunshine through
Delighted by the sight of you
Relaxed with breaths of fragrant blooms
So dear to honey bees.

We'll sit here for an hour or so
And watch the humming birds and sky
And as the moving clouds go by
We'll dream our dreams and symphonize
The pleasing forms before our eyes
Beneath this graceful linden tree
The perfect place for you and me.

GOLDSMITH'S HAMMER

It is gone, forever gone,
The rhythm of his hammer
On the metal at his bench.

His daily songs of shaping
Joyful songs of making
Precious metal ringing
On the anvil near his bench.

His hands were made for work
Impassioned lean and strong
Eyes quick and focused
A mind intent responding

To the challenge of his metal
A métier loved rebounding
With the rhythm of a hammer
In the forging of a life.

PASSAGE

My loss remains a desert
    of shifting sands
Rocks pulverized by sun and wind
    obscure my path.
There is no soothing rain
There is no fog to cloth my
    nakedness and ease my suffering.
Powers that be in deep and silent emptiness,
Release my heart to overcome
    the tyranny of Mind
    the apathy of time
    Restore the sweetest confidence
    in present life sublimed.

IN MY SEEING I BEHOLD

In my seeing I behold
The bounty of the trees
The faithfulness of doves
The ordered life of bees
The daily work of love
The power of the tide
The bracing of the wind
The mysteries of the deep
The folding wings of sleep.

Further Reading

Aymar, Brandt, and Edward Sagarin. *A Pictorial History of The World's Great Trials: From Socrates to Jean Harris.* New York: Bonanza Books, 1985.

Cheney, Sheldon. *The Story of Modern Art.* New York: The Viking Press, 1941.

Clark, Kenneth. *The Nude: A Study in Ideal Form.* Princeton, NJ: Princeton University Press, 1956.

De Mille, Agnes. *The Book of Dance.* New York: Golden Press, 1963.

Dewey, John. "Morals and Conduct" from *Human Nature and Conduct: An Introduction to Social Psychology.* In *Man and Man: The Social Philosophers.* Ed. Saxe Commins and Robert N. Linscott. New York: Random House, 1947.

Dickler, Gerald, *Man On Trial: History-making Trials from Socrates to Oppenheimer.* Garden City, NY: Doubleday, 1962.

Donovan, Frank Robert. *The Vikings.* New York: American Heritage Pub. Co., 1964.

Horst, Louis and Carroll Russell. *Modern Dance Forms: In Relation to the Other Modern Arts.* 1961. Reprint, Hightstown, NJ: Princeton Book Company, 1987.

Horst, Louis. *Pre-Classic Dance Forms.* 1937. Reprint, Hightstown, NJ: Princeton Book Company, 1987.

Huyghe, Rene. *Ideas and Images in World Art: Dialogue with the Visible.* New York: Harry N. Abrams, Inc., 1959.

Kessel, Dmitri, and Henri Peyre. *Splendors of Christendom: Great Art and Architecture in European Churches.* Lausanne: Edita S.A. Lausanne, 1964.

Leatherman, Leroy. *Martha Graham.* New York: Alfred A. Knopf, 1966.

McClinton, Katherine Morrison. *Christian Church Art through the Ages.* New York: The Macmillan Company, 1962.

Morgan, Barbara. *Martha Graham*. Philadelphia and New York: Beck Engraving Company, 1941.

Maurois, Andre. *A History of France*. Trans. Henry L. Binsse and Gerard Hopkins. New York: Farrar, Straus and Cudahy, 1956.

Preminger, Alex, T. V. F. Brogan, O. B. Hardison Jr., and Earl Miner, eds. *The New Princeton Encyclopedia of Poetry and Poetics*. Princeton: Princeton University Press, 1993.

Skolle, John. *Azalaï*. New York: Harper & Brothers, 1955.

Switzer, Ellen. *Dancers! Horizons in American Dance*. New York: Atheneum, 1982.

Time-Life Books. *The World in Arms: Timeframe AD 1900–1925*. Richmond, VA: The Time Inc. Book Company, 1989.

Thompson, Daniel V. *The Practice of Tempura Painting*. New Haven, CT: Yale University Press, 1936.

Index